A Dream Come True

By
Jeryn Alise Turner

Jeryn Alise Turner Books are available for order through Ingram Press Catalogues

Jeryn A. Turner

Visit my website at www.jerynturner.com

Printed in the United States of America

First Printing: April 2016

Published by Sojourn Publishing, LLC

ISBN: 978-1-62747-224-1
eBook ISBN: 978-1-62747-225-8

Acknowledgements

I would like to express my deep and loving gratitude to my family. My Grandfather taught me responsibility, my Great Uncle taught me humility and my Grandmother showed me unconditional love and sacrifice. My grandmother and I were very close and shared a special bond. She had a significant impact on my life and always saw the best in me. I also share this experience with all the amazing people in my life; my mentees, numerous mentors, friends, supporters and fellow writers. I appreciate you asking me about the book and keeping me accountable. Your cards, phone calls, text messages and constant encouragement turned my dream into a reality.

The adoration from two very special women gave me the confidence to write this book, Laura Anderson and Barbara Love Postell. You both will be forever in my heart and I am grateful for the influence you had on my life. I would be remiss if I didn't mention my parents, my sisters, brother, cousins, aunts, uncles and close family friends. My mother is an amazing woman and shaped my views about everything. Although fiction, I used this book to showcase the great advice given to me over the years. My family has always believed in me and showed up when I needed them. They see my unlimited potential and undiscovered gifts. Because of them I believe that anything is possible and I can do anything. I am grateful for their approachability, love, humor, wit, inspiration, and reassurance. They are living examples of God's grace. My niece and nephew changed my life. They motivate me in ways that no one else can. I want to be my best so I can give them my all. They bring bright color to my life and encourage me to love incessantly.

This book is dedicated to my mother. Thank you for giving me the gift of life and demonstrating the power of the human spirit.

Contents

The Invitation

"On the day that you were born the angels got together and decided to create a dream come true. So, they sprinkled moon dust in your hair... Just like me, they long to be close to you." I know this Karen Carpenter song very well; every year my mother calls and sings it on my birthday. This year I missed her call because I was at the gym longer than expected. Once my yoga teacher found out it was my birthday she bought me a smoothie and we talked about my plans for the day. I usually do something big for my birthday but this year I was content having dinner with a few friends. After listening to mom serenade me on voice mail, I called her back. She picked up the phone immediately and continued singing. As I listen to her I wonder if it is just my family who has these annual traditions or if others do the same.

But this year, after singing this song, she says something that I don't expect. "I want to celebrate my next birthday with you in Peru." I am surprised when I hear these words. I am not surprised about the destination, since my mother has visited every continent except for Antarctica. Although an avid traveler, we have not traveled together internationally. I am a little shocked because she is asking me, and not going with one of her friends or her husband. After high school, family vacations are usually replaced by spring break blow-outs, honeymoons, romantic trips, and the timeless girlfriend vacations. This would be the first time as an adult that we would be together – uninterrupted and alone –for a full two weeks.

Travel has always been how my mother has chosen to escape. She comes alive on her trips, not being confined to her routine lifestyle, but instead opening herself up to whatever intriguing thing may present itself: zip-lining, language classes, mountain climbing, dinner with the locals and more. She works so that she can travel, and each year she picks a foreign land to explore. Regardless of her obligations, vacations have been her pleasure; her first trip was to Puerto Rico, shortly after having my older sister. I think people were surprised that a new mother would make that kind of trip alone, but she did. And she has embarked on a similar adventure every year – sometimes taking multiple trips. Some people dream about amazing vacations but annually my mom lives out her wildest dream, letting her heart dictate her path.

I didn't inherit her same level of independence. I travel, but usually my trips involve a beach, some wine and a few girlfriends. The only trip I took alone was to a bed-and-breakfast in the mountains to clear my head. I only ventured out to go to my spa treatments and fitness classes. My meals were included, so I didn't have to deal with the uncomfortable stares one often receives when dining alone. I guess such things don't bother my mother, or maybe she is oblivious to the looks. She has done a lot of things alone recently, since relocating for her career five years ago.

She moved to Washington, DC by herself to take the Chief Marketing Officer role with an ad agency. A promotion that allowed her financial security and flexibility since the position came with an executive team. While there she started working out more, took up healthy cooking and reconnected with friends from college. One of which who invited her to visit their church, Mt. Olive Missionary Church. She would visit often and after the annual Easter play, she decided to inquire more about their drama department, which led her to join the church. One of the first things she did was start attending all the drama events, plays and practices. After a few rehearsals, she was cast as Mary, the star of the Christmas play. This experience reminded her how much she missed the thrill of the stage. She loved the spotlight and enjoyed working with people with similar passion. She was grateful that she had found her first love. People complimented her gift and it was a good outlet of stress for her. After practice, one of her costars gave her the information to their acting coach. She walked around with that card in her purse for months until one night she stumbled upon it while aimlessly watching TV. She hadn't called earlier because she was still transitioning into the new role; now her schedule is predictable. Most evenings she was out of work by 6:30 and found herself filling time with books, movies, dinners with friends or watching TV. After an initial consultation, they both agreed that mom had talent and her acting coach known as Ms. May began meeting with her once a week on Wednesday evenings.

Her sessions led to finding out about commercials, voice over work and local plays; she was even casted in a few local productions. She enjoyed the rigor of practice and the close intimacy she developed with her fellow thespians. My family would often go to DC for her performances and we noticed her elevated happiness and joy. She would always join us for holidays and we would frequently visit her for vacations. My step dad quickly grew accustomed to going to her place for long weekends. My younger brother had just started college when she relocated so he wasn't forced to adjust to the new family set up; the living arrangement quickly became our new normal.

She frequently traveled to New York City for business and would always find time to attend Broadway shows. While there she dreamed that she would be discovered on the street for having the right look. During one of her many business trips, her best friend decided to meet her there. After a couple bottles of red wine she convinced mom to reach out to a local talent agent she knew. Since our cousin is in the music business she called him and he confirmed the agent was great at placing "seasoned new talent". After contacting the agent, she was convinced to try out for the Off Broadway Show *Momma I Want to Sing!* a show she had seen 20 years ago during a couple's trip with good friends from Cincinnati, Ohio.

To everyone's surprise she landed a lead role in the show. She was excited about the opportunity but also realized she couldn't be available for practices in NY while working a day job. She talked to her colleagues and learned that after 5 years employees are eligible to apply for a sabbatical. The timing also worked out financially since my brother recently graduated from college and the family house was paid off. Before committing to the play we had a meeting to discuss her plans and the impact on the family. She applied for the sabbatical and within two weeks it was approved. She focused her energy on getting her affairs in order to move yet again. Most of her items were shipped home but she kept her favorite clothes, a few sentimental pictures, her bedroom suite, and her prized possessions; her books. Books by Marianne Williamson, Maya Angelou, Louise Hay and Don Miguel Ruiz fill mom's nightstand and mind. These individuals have been credited with this generation's spiritual revolution and I believe are the catalyst behind her recent change and enlightenment.

For a woman who has been surrounded by people her whole life – she is the third oldest of a family of six, and had her first child shortly after finishing college. Alone time was a rarity. Now she was living in her dream city on her own terms. She was excited as if she had been reborn. It was funny to hear her talk about new restaurants, and learning how to use the subway – things I could relate to, since I have spent time in New York for internships and business travel. Where my mother has probably struggled over the years with how to have her own space, I always have "me time," easily escaping life by simply coming home. Mom, however, has not had such a luxury in life until recently. While I was growing up, everyone depended on her – us kids, her husband, her family – so she always had to be responsible, never doing things "just because." Every decision had to be considered for the consequences they created for the family as a whole. Every new job had to be analyzed: How much money will I get? Is it stable? Can I move up?

She wouldn't have considered making this type of change when she was younger – now she does, because she has more confidence. I am surprised that this confidence took her so long to develop. I have always looked up to my mother; she is a beautiful woman with very strong features. When she was growing up, everyone tried to claim her as their own; Native Americans, Latinos, Ethiopians and even Asians. Her high cheekbones, slanted eyes, sandy brown curly hair and statuesque height made her stand out. Her fluency in Spanish, French and Portuguese also made her exotic. People wanted to see themselves in her because she was smart, intriguing and talented. To be associated with her fine qualities made them feel better about themselves.

Mom was competitive, naturally quick and athletic; never backing down from a challenge or game. She knew she would easily win against girls, and when it came to the guys, she knew if they wanted to win they would have to work for it. I was surprised to learn that she was not actually as confident as what I thought she projected. I would later find out that she'd had a lot of confidence growing up – but that bad relationships robbed her of that self-assurance. At her core she knew she was able, but over time she let people into her life – mainly men who were not good for her and allowed their thinking to become her thinking. Years of this chipped away at her dreams – and that is why it took her so long to believe that she could become the singer and actor that she always dreamed of.

As a recent "empty nester," my mother is figuring out how to spend her time, remembering interests that she had sacrificed and learning how to reprioritize. I can relate to her because I am at a similar crossroad, making some major life changes regarding my career and what I want out of life. Most women my age are getting married and starting to have children, and I feel out of touch with this reality. I feel like my invitation just showed up for a party that everyone else has been attending for years. Just like my mother, I've been able, by being alone, to take more risks in life – freeing up my time, finances and energy to pour into my soul and the things I find important. Mom often referred to her solo time as growth periods, still loving her family but desperately needing to figure out something in her life that can only come from focused solitude. Now that all of her kids are grown, and some of them have started families of their own, mom feels she has the freedom to do things that she always wanted – which includes taking a trip to Peru with me.

As I think about her invitation, my mind reflects on the relationship we have had over the years – the good times, the trying times and the times when things just didn't make sense. Mom and I butted heads over boys, going out, grades, and how I spent my free time. She worked very long hours, I considered her a workaholic and felt like my time with her took a backseat to her high powered job. I always felt like I was competing with my siblings, her friends, social calendar or inner drive for more. To compensate for her late hours and high standards, she was strict, much stricter than I would have liked. She took pride in having a respectful kid who got good grades and followed the rules. Although my childhood was uneventful, I missed having a special closeness with my mother. I think every child wishes for what they didn't have, assuming their life would be better or magically transformed if they had what they believe they lacked. As a successful woman who turned out well, I realize that she did the best she could, but growing up I didn't always have that same type of emotional maturity.

While in school, everything always went back to GPA, which was considered the Holy Grail in my house. Since I thought that was the only thing that mattered then, I wondered if she loved me unconditionally, or if the measure of love she extended was based on my grades and what I did. A = time with my friends, dinners out, special treats, and compliments; B = less TV watching and free time; C = housework, chores to be done on the weekends, don't even ask to do anything with your friends and extra babysitting duty; D = punishment, always being questioned about what I was doing, feeling stressed about everything, F = I wasn't crazy enough to see what type of treatment this would warrant – I knew it was bad and didn't want any part of it.

I hated being evaluated for everything I did or said, or how I acted. I wanted to be supported by her and not feel everything I did had to be justified by career aspirations, purpose or a business plan. I wanted to be able to relax with her and not feel like everything had to be scheduled. I wanted her to teach me beauty lessons, how to put on make-up, and how to be girly. I wanted her to share with me how to live a well-adjusted life –

which includes having an outlet. She taught me exceptional professional skills; creating a tenacious, highly educated daughter. But I have always struggled with balance, never really allowing myself to fully unwind. I use a calendar to plan out my social time, filling it with things I enjoy, but sometimes I wonder if they are turning into obsessions. I expected my mother to teach me all the tools for success, including how to be prosperous – but also how to have peace.

As a young girl, I wanted my mom to be different. She worked very hard, so I wished I'd had a stay-at-home mom. My grandmother cooked all of the time, so I wanted my mom to cook and bake everything from scratch. I loved to dance and cheerlead, and so I prayed that she would become a cheer mom. I longed for a mom who was passionate about my interests and invested time in those things. I idolized all the moms who waited for the kids during practice and worked the concession stand during the games. I wanted the supermom that everyone knew, and thought was cool. There is a mom I remember fondly who fit that bill, Debby Lewis. She was the type of mom who was always around. I would find a reason to talk to her just so I could be near her. In my child's mind, she was the epitome of what a mother should be. It didn't matter how she was at home with her own kids or husband; I didn't care what she did professionally. Since everyone adored her I did too; in my eyes she was perfect. Since she represented perfection, I looked at my own mother differently, putting more emphasis on the things that she didn't do and always focusing on what I thought she lacked.

Even though I knew my mother wasn't Debby, I expected her to change. I thought that she sensed my dissatisfaction; I hoped she would go to the magical shop where mothers are made and get a tune-up. My unspoken expectations were not met; so any attempts she made were never enough and went unnoticed and unacknowledged. When she cooked dinner I was looking for the homemade rolls. When she made dessert I was looking for homemade ice-cream and cookies cut into cartoon characters. When she took us roller-skating I wished we went more often. When she came to football games I wished she cheered louder.

In hindsight, I am wondering if I put too many expectations on her to be my everything. Her most important job was to make sure I was protected, which she did; that I was financially cared for, which she took care of; that I was loved, which I knew; and that I was supported, which I always was. Whatever I thought my mother lacked in providing I got from my aunt, my sister and my grandmother, who were always available, so I never went without. Years later I question why I expected her to fill all of my needs, especially since her extended support group was able. I always knew she had dreams outside of just being a wife and mother, so growing up I didn't want to be her burden. She didn't want me to be anyone else's burden either, so she made sure I didn't have to depend on anyone outside of the family.

I think most moms want their daughters to be independent, but my mom's fixation on this topic skewed my ability to accept help from others. I looked at niceness with cautious eyes, assuming that anyone who extends themselves has ulterior motives. When it came to men, I assumed there was manipulation behind every action, word, or amiable offering. I know there had to be a good reason for why she raised me in this way, but I am not sure of her motive. She was a young mother and had two children before I was born. My memories start when my mother remarried and within 18 months my younger brother was born. There were lots of changes in a short span of time, with no mention of why things were happening, but instead a rush on adjusting and making sure the new pieces of our life fit together. There really was no discussion of how these changes made us feel, or an acknowledgement of what transpired. We were constantly told to be on our best behavior as though we were auditioning to play ourselves in the remake of our family.

No one talked about the past, it was never discussed. We learned to follow our parents' lead and act like everything was ok even if we felt uncertainty. Since they didn't create an open space for dialogue, we didn't think open dialogue was something that should be done, which created a fear of questioning. There were many times when I wanted to hear my mother's thoughts about something, or ask her about her feelings, but we were told to stay out of grown folks' business – especially when we saw adults talking. I wanted to hear about the pivotal moments in her life, so I could know her as a person and not just a mother. I assumed that if you don't talk about something, then there must be a story worth hiding, and the answer that you may receive is not worth the pain instigated by the question. I learned to be socially ignorant but scholastically intelligent, since grades were so important. Ironically I would openly question things in the classroom, but closed off my inquisitive nature when it came to relationships of any kind, a trait that I would carry into my adult life.

I accepted what was given and learned to be selfless almost to the point of being invisible. I sacrificed myself in the hope of getting what I thought I wanted without expressing what I needed. Why is it, as "good" daughters, we take everyone else's opinions of our life as being worth more than our own? Why is it, as "good" daughters, that we have been trained to follow without questioning? Being a "good daughter" is an admirable role to play when you live with your parents – but it is something that you must switch off when you interact with others who may not have your best interests at heart. The attributes of unquestioned devotion that you have as a child are the very things that you must work to undo as you mature.

My greatest wakeup calls were when I found myself in situations that depleted me as a person, and made me think it was okay to settle and accept less. I have always struggled with feeling needy when interacting with others – a feeling that I think comes from asking others to do what I should be doing for myself. I am frustrated with myself for shifting responsibility in the hopes of fulfillment, yet still feeling deprived. I am comfortable playing the submissive role, and my default was to play that role in many aspects of my life: professionally, socially, and romantically. It is a role that allowed me to evade blame, putting most of the emphasis on the actions of others. Relationships are hard but when someone shuts down they are impossible to manage. I would disengage when I felt the other person was becoming emotionally distant and not open. I could have communicated my feelings but I was afraid of the answer so I let things gradually fade away.

This has negatively impacted my romantic relationships. Either the person would grow tired of trying to figure out what I was thinking, or I would grow tired of suppressing my spirit. I wanted to be more expressive, wishing I could go after what I wanted in life. For far too long, I had been passive about things that mattered to me. I needed to show up for myself in all areas and pursue what interested me most. My biggest apprehension is being placed in situations where I am not ready and hurting or disappointing those that depend on me. So I played it safe rather than push myself to try something different. I also know I am emotionally sensitive and for the majority of my life have tried to hide this from other people, especially men. I conceal my feelings because I want to appear cool even when I'm not.

My mother has always called me her emotional child. A label that I didn't see as positive because she rarely showed hers. Growing up, I felt weak so instead of expressing myself I was quiet. My whole life, I've wanted my mother to validate that my feelings were normal. So many things are blamed on hormones with little regard for how situations impact our lives. I wanted to hear my emotions were real and what I felt was justified. That I can overcome heartbreak because she has been me and come out on the other side with grace.

I want her to look at me and feel comfortable talking about her past, and not dwell on what I shouldn't be doing – but tell me instead, based on her own experiences, *why* I shouldn't do such things. I don't want her to preach from her usual moral high road because she knows where the road I am on can lead or because she is trying to step in front of the emotional crash that I am headed for. I want her to humbly relate to me as a woman, and not as my guardian; as someone who has feelings and a heart, and not as a shell of a woman who feels she must always hold things together. For once I want her to be vulnerable with me, so that together we can put the pieces of our hearts together. For once, I want her to trust me enough to show me the complexity of her spirit and life. As I pack for my trip, I am consciously remembering and unleashing many emotions I have carried around for so many years of my life. Silent wishes and hopes for a deeper connection, secrets I never shared with my mother – and secrets I suspect she never shared with me.

I find that secrets between mothers and daughters are very common. Mothers try to portray themselves as perfect; like they have always operated in the way they instruct their daughters. Daughters feel they can't live up to this perfection, because their flaws are easily noticed and addressed by their mothers. Daughters develop a love/hate relationship with their mothers. Loving them for the life they have been given but hating them for parenting them under a microscope; always looking for teachable moments instead of tender ones. This type of pressure-based parenting makes daughters retaliate by looking for faults in their mothers. In an effort to even out the playing field and not feel so bad about themselves, daughters start keeping a list of their mothers' flaws; vowing to be different.

So when daughters become adults, they work hard to hide anything that is seen as less than perfect or can cause worry. Both parties are seeking validation from each other but are afraid to be vulnerable, and these superficial relationships cause both mothers and daughters to suffer in silence. Why is it so hard for mothers to tell their daughters about times in their lives where they have made mistakes? And why can't daughters open up to their mothers about problems they have before they become major issues requiring intervention?

The mother-daughter relationship is one of the most sacred of all connections, but often one of the most fragile, because of the confusion regarding boundaries. Daughters' feel they are the only source of joy for their mother if the mother lived a selfless life. In these situations, daughters feel selfish when they do things for themselves or go against their mother's wishes. Daughters are also afraid to be honest about their views of what it means to be a wife and mother, especially if those differ from what they have been taught. Today daughters are choosing not to marry or getting married much later. They are deciding to wait before having children and often doing it alone. The concept of marriage has changed and for the sake of inner peace, many have decided to redefine it to fit their needs. Options have increased for women as they find and exercise their independence. As progressive as our society appears, old thoughts concerning the roles of women are slow to catch up to these modern-day trends. Mothers and daughters are put in a tough position as they struggle to relate and see things from each other's point of view.

Instead of being honest and having a healthy dialogue, conversations are minimized to "safe topics" such as work, home improvement projects, recipes, and the news. Daughters often recite common catch phrases like "I'm fine," "Work is great," and "Life is good" when asked a question, while secretly hiding a sense of disconnection when it comes to expressing real emotions. Parents, especially mothers, feel they need to portray a type of idealized role model to get the attention and respect of their daughters, making daughters feel more like treasured assets rather than figures of love. And at the core of any mother's relationship, she feels responsible for her daughters' safety and success, a burden that is hard to manage – especially as her daughter grows into adulthood and wants to make her own decisions.

All mothers want to protect their daughters from pain, but often struggle with how to balance development with disappointment. There is a level of understanding that can only be achieved by allowing someone to feel all of the highs and lows of life. But it's often hard for a mother to watch that process take place, because at the core, a mother hates to see her child in pain. Just like the lioness protecting her cubs, the mother is always in protective mode, sensing pain to stop it before it happens. Although the mother knows that overcoming such situations builds the daughter's confidence and character, the inner fear of every mother is that maybe her daughter is not strong enough to survive if things take a turn for the worse. All mothers have high hopes for their daughters, wishing that they will have the best life, and hoping only for their success. Since there is no special rulebook that comes with parenting, it's a job often learned by trial and error. Some things work, and other things can be done better. Mothers and daughters are learning together throughout this process, and adapting to ever-changing circumstances.

Every daughter hopes that her mother's true feelings are expressed, and that they don't hide behind "shoulds." I have observed some of the worst mother/daughter fights; arguments about the actions of a daughter. Based on the type of pain expressed by the mother I know it's deeper than what has happened and has triggered something from the past, reinjuring an old wound. For the sake of the relationship, mothers and daughters will have to go to that place and reach a type of honesty that is not always common. To truly move past a disagreement, you have to be truthful about what caused the disappointment and explosive reaction. Strict mothers are often scared mothers who fear that someone or something will take away their daughter's joy; controlling mothers have been hurt, and wish for their children to avoid the pain that they still carry. Overbearing mothers try to live out their lives through their daughters, often sacrificing everything – including their life – so that their daughters can have the world.

Mothers often put undue pressure on daughters because of what they were not able to accomplish in their own lives. Daughters are given an opportunity to live, but often only within the parameters that mothers design. Daughters will grow up too, and even then, mothers have a hard time letting go – not because they don't like the person before them, but because they are not ready to transition to a relationship of equal power. Mothers are not disappointed when daughters choose differently; they just don't want their offspring to know the pain that comes with life – and since they have lived longer, they know how things work. If possible, they want to keep their daughters safe and innocent. If mothers could make a deal with the devil to remain in labor throughout the lives of their daughters, they would do that, if that meant that their girls would not know pain or suffering. Over time, mothers eventually come around, because they realize that the relationship is more important than the dispute. Mothers want their daughters is to remember what they were taught about forgiveness and to apply it to all people – including themselves.

Tensions flare when expectations are not met, and disputes are more about what the desired outcome should be, rather than the subject of dissension itself. When a fight/ disagreement/ argument – whatever you want to call it – comes up, the best thing a daughter can do is to let her mother talk without interruption. The first response to a disagreement is usually anger and a need to be defensive, which is counterproductive to talking and working towards a resolution. If both parties are trying to maintain the relationship, then it's important to remain levelheaded. Words said in anger are usually the only words remembered. Being quiet is not agreeing to what has been said; being quiet is a tactful tool to understand the other person's perspective and see why they feel the way they feel. Disagreements are more about the feelings ignited within than about what the other person has to say or what they have done.

There will always be friction between mothers and daughters because both are wired the same; sharing the same fuse that can either fuel passion or trigger explosive emotions. They know what will upset the other because it is usually what upsets them. The blessing in this relationship is that they also know what will heal the other because they are created from the same place. Mothers give their daughters life at birth, but if a mother is able to restore her daughter's spirit as an adult, the relationship is tighter than any other that exists here on Earth.

More than anything, mothers want to feel they have done their job as a parent. They are in charge of their children's development, but ultimately a parent's success is based on how their children turn out. People look at parents and either give accolades, or criticism based on their own judgments. There is no universal definition of success; everything – is *subjective.* Mothers and daughters play similar roles in each other's lives, and interchangeably role-play to be the champion and hero; roles that facilitate growth during challenging times. It doesn't stop when a daughter turns eighteen. By law, she is an adult then, but every mother knows that her daughter will always be her baby, no matter what the birth certificate says. When she leaves home, the training wheels come off – and mothers hope that daughters continue to hear their trusted voices, and the lessons they planted in their minds.

Daughters wish to have genuine relationships with their mothers, giving anything to hear their stories. The road to adulthood has its fair share of bumps, bruises and scars. As we experience difficulties, we need to hear this road has a destination. Words are easily forgotten, but memories are bonded when two people let down their walls and connect on an emotional level. Daughters want a place to go where mistakes can be made without chastising, and where decisions don't need justification. Where daughters are implicitly trusted to live a good life, and where daughters don't have to worry about consulting their mothers on every decision. We need our mothers to not only believe in us, but also in our ability to make decisions and take care of ourselves. Daughters will always need their mothers, but the best relationships are the ones that develop and morph over time. Where mothers are not judged unfairly for past decisions made, and where daughters are given free license to create their future without worry of disappointment. The beauty of seeing each other at the same point in time is that the past and future don't matter. The present is all that exists, and without the baggage of memories or worries, mothers and daughters can relate on the same level. This is what I hope my mom and I can do on this trip.

The Trip

My mom flies in the day before our flight leaves for Peru. I have been cleaning to prepare for her visit, because I want her to think that my life is in order. I want to show her how good my life is, and how I have been able to develop into a person capable of taking care of herself. A clean house does not mean that everything is okay, but I want to appear pristine so that she doesn't dig deeper into how I am feeling, or what I am dealing with. I am not ready to tell her about the secret relationship drama I have been dealing with, and how a guy I fell for has been treating me like I am invisible. I am not ready to get deep with her because I know I will cry – and I want to be able to hold it together at least until we get out of the country.

We arrive in Peru very late, after traveling for just about six hours. When we land, we assume that taxis would be lined up waiting for us. But just as in every other country, corruption exists, and the airport has commercialized the taxi system. After we prepay for our taxi service, we walk outside and present our ticket to the next available cabby. It helps that my mother is fluent in Spanish, so she is quickly able to communicate the location of our hotel. After understanding a few words that are exchanged I close my eyes, and the next thing I know, we've arrived at the hotel. When planning this trip, we only booked two nights in the main city of Lima. Mom wanted to get out into the countryside and interact with the natives. We figured we would stay a few nights in the plush hotel while figuring out where the indigenous people lived.

The next day, since I got ample sleep on the plane and on the way to the hotel, I got up and went up to the rooftop pool while mom slept in. I left her a note on the nightstand, letting her know where I was, since I didn't want her to worry – especially since I don't remember very much of the Spanish I learned years ago. While at the pool I struck up a good conversation with an Australian chiropractor who used to live in Peru, and who was in the city with his girlfriend and her family. When I told him what type of adventure mom was looking for, he quickly outlined the places we needed to visit. He said that everyone who comes to Peru needs to see Machu Picchu, but also recommended Agua Caliente (Hot Springs), Sacred Valley, Cuzco and Ollantaytambo. He told me that if we wanted to visit Machu Picchu we would have to take a plane, train and bus to get to the mountain. We were staying in Lima, so we would have to meet with a travel agent to book tickets to Cuzco. He recommended a few well-known travel agents, and suggested that I ask the hotel where the closest agency was located. I didn't know that Peru had so many interesting places to visit. Mom was the one who wanted to go to Peru, so unlike with other trips, I didn't take time to research this country, or the places I should visit. I was comfortable with letting my mother take the reins. I trusted that just as she did when I was young, she would lead the way.

Since mom has been peacefully relaxing – or should I say sleeping – for the past four hours, I figured it was time to check on her and update her on the information that my new Australian friend had just given me. By the time I went downstairs to check on mom, she was dressed and had gone down to the restaurant. I joined her for brunch. Ceviche is a popular dish in Peru, so that was brought out first. She smiled as I told her about my new comrade, because she knows I will talk to anyone even when I'm in a foreign land. We were both excited to be in Peru, and we wanted to try all the new delicacies that were presented to us at brunch. I have been gluten free for almost four years, so mom had to explain to our server what I was able to eat. She reassured us that since the staple grains in Peru are quinoa, yucca and corn; I shouldn't have any issues. I became very good at saying "Soy alérgico al trigo" which means I have a wheat allergy. During our brunch we talked about many random things. Even though I've known my mother all my life this was the first time I found out that that she was a big baby, weighing over nine pounds at birth. If I didn't know about her birth and introduction into this world, what else didn't I know about?

After brunch we asked the hotel where the closest travel agent was, then headed there to book the rest of our time in Peru. We decided on the nine-day package, which included a week in Cuzco and two days for travel. The excursions we selected included tours of museums, homes, huts, churches, burial grounds, temples, and markets in the Sacred Valley, Agua Calientes, and Ollantaytambo. Our trip ended with a 3 day hiking trip to Machu Picchu. We had a full two weeks planned, and we were both feeling pretty excited about what our time would entail. Since mom had bought our tickets to Peru I decided that I would surprise her with purchasing the vacation package. She actually got off easy, since the excursions was two-thirds of the total cost.

When we left the agency I saw a familiar name, Pinkberry. I used to eat this yogurt all the time while living in New York, and since mom recently moved there she is familiar with its goodness. I hadn't eaten it in a few years so it was ironic that I had to travel all the way to Peru to get a taste of one of my favorite treats. Mom decided that she would treat me, the least she could do for my recent investment into Peru's GDP. Later that night, we enjoyed an authentic dinner of quinoa, yucca and fire roasted chicken skewers with a side of avocado and tomato. After dinner we packed since our flight was leaving for Cuzco early the next day.

Sacred Valley

One of the first stops we made after flying to Cuzco and checking into the hotel was to the Sacred Valley. We were on the bus for three hours, and I was happy to arrive. The air conditioner made my fingers look and feel like ice cubes; I'm now ready to walk around so I can stretch my legs. The first thing I do is look up to the sky and allow the sun to beat down on my face, so that its heat can warm me up from the inside out. The warmness that is flowing throughout my body gives me a sense of calmness. I start to feel at peace even though I am in a foreign place. There is something soothing about the sun and sky; they come with you wherever you go so you never feel that you are traveling alone. I walk around to an old hut that has been around since the beginning of the civilization and sit down on a smooth rock, first sitting, then stretching. Before I know it, I am in a warrior pose, and I have begun to replay my yoga routine from memory. I have just taken up the practice, so some of the positions are not smooth yet, but it feels good to stretch in this moment. I stop to take a drink of water, since I have worked up a sweat and I sit down on that same rock that inspired me to stretch. I want to feel the sun on my arms, so I take off my jacket and lie down. The next thing I remember is hearing the following words: "I am proud of you."

Since the other people who traveled with us from the tour have gone ahead, I know this voice has to be my mother's. Her voice sounds different – calmer and lighter so I open my eyes to make sure it's her. It's mom but she looks much younger. I recognize her, but I no longer see the mature woman wearing a black jogging suit with sneakers that I had breakfast with this morning. She looks just like her graduation picture from high school – a picture taken when she was eighteen. I know this image well because it has been on display in my grandmother's living room for as long as I can remember. Mom's body is slim and tall, almost model-esque. Her hair is naturally curly and styled in a big sandy brown afro that brushes her shoulders. She is wearing bell bottoms with a half shirt showing a very small and flat tummy. The glasses that I am used to seeing are gone. Her style is youthful and fun. She is sitting on the rock near me with her legs crossed, and her eyes are squinting because the sun is out and very bright.

Confused by what I am seeing I am thinking that I drank too much Pisco Sour the night before, or maybe I am experiencing some serious altitude sickness and my body and mind have not adjusted to being up so high. I am puzzled that my mother would show up in a form that I am not used to seeing. Not a wife. Not a career woman. Not my teacher – but as a young woman. A young woman who I am ashamed to say I don't really know, since my whole life I have looked at my mom as my protector, the one to call on when I am in need. My mom is great in emergencies, not letting emotions take over but being practical about solutions. Seeing her at a younger age makes me see her as much more vulnerable and open, which is a different look for my mom. I was taught that vulnerability is a sign of weakness, and even when you feel like you are struggling, you need to put on a brave face. In my family, you never want to be played a fool, so we were taught to keep our image intact even if we were hurting. Everyone assumes that the women in our family have it together – because that is what we want others to see, controlling our emotions so they don't control us, and never letting strangers into family business.

But in her younger state, she has a lightness about her that I have not seen recently. Her skin is glowing. She is looking at me as if she can almost see through me, but instead of feeling uneasy, as though she knows I have done something wrong, her glare makes me feel comfortable. As I look at the young woman standing before me I don't know much about this person: my memories of her start on the day I was born. I have always been curious to understand her thoughts about dating, relationships, and life. When we talk about these topics it's usually when I am upset, and so this turns her focus on what the other person has done, and less on what I could have done differently. When I was young her focus was taking us to church and making sure we received a good education. I studied really hard during the school year, and read books in the summer. There was little time spent with her sharing emotional details about the growing pains that she faced.

Eighteen is a milestone age, the point where children leave the comforts of home and begin to make decision without the direct guidance of parents. Since I see her as a person who can relate to me, and not as a perfectly assembled mother figure, I feel more relaxed around her. I feel she is more authentic and won't give me the textbook "mother" response, like when I have asked her questions before. I want to tap into the place in her heart that hasn't been made bitter by bad relationships, divorce or disappointment. I hope that she speaks with innocence and remembers the time when she believed anything was possible; when she believed in fairy tales. I want to engage, and see if that place lives within her – because it still lives within me. I want to ask her about what she did to feel comfortable in her own skin physically, emotionally – and more importantly, spiritually.

Ironically enough, Peru is known for his spiritual mysticism. There are few places on Earth this strong with a long lineage of known shamans and healers. A place that draws visitors not only with its breathtaking views, but with the spiritual energy it offers those who are open to experience it. Peru is a place where the culture remains strong through the stories of its people, and it attracts those who seek to move forward on their path of self-mastery and awareness. The region includes the Andes Mountains, which are considered to represent high dimensions of power. Peru is known for its ancient culture and heritage. The Incas are the most known civilization associated with Peru, especially with Machu Picchu. They not only contributed to the landscape of the country but also created a foundation for strong beliefs. There is a powerful spiritual presence felt when you visit places like the Sacred Valley and Machu Picchu.

Peru is one of the rare places where the early architecture is still preserved to this day. When you visit the country, you can see the ancient huts and the ways that the indigenous people lived. Elsewhere, the evidence of history might no longer exist, but in Peru it is different; you can clearly see and visit many of these age-old structures. There are constant reminders of how advanced and knowledgeable these people were. They were able to create sanctuaries that are still intact today, able to move rocks weighing over a ton without the use of a crane, and able to create solar-powered gardens. The things they were able to do still defy logic, and modern scientists don't understand which has opened their minds to other options. Peru has to be spiritual because realistically, nothing else makes sense. Being connected to something bigger than life is the only way to explain how they were able to thrive in the way they did. The ancient cultures of Peru were very centered, always paying homage to their gods and developing a civilization around their beliefs.

When you visit a place so rich in faith, grounded in the souls of its people and the power of the land, you know you have encountered something sacred. The type of sacredness that creates a pureness of spirit within and awakens aspects of your life long forgotten. The type of energy that connects you with the beauty of nature. The magic of Peru lies in what its people were able to accomplish. It motivates you to look at your own resources not just to survive, but to use what you have been blessed with to thrive. Peru is timeless because the truth that the ancestors believed in has been passed down to its modern-day residents. Truth that is still relevant today. The people of Peru believe in the goodness of people, working together as a community and helping their fellow man. That is the only way they lived and the only way we will live. Peru reminds us that the best of life is not always in front of us; it reminds us to respect our past and leverage and use what we have inherited. Peru raises your awareness of what you think is possible – because this land stretches possibilities. You begin to do the same in your life and believe in dreams that you once felt silly for having. It's a magical place because the impossible, inconceivable and unexplainable actually happen here. It draws many people because they are hoping that the magic will rub off in their own lives, and that they can take with them the strength and power found throughout the country.

Especially in the Sacred Valley – an amazing place, full of golden mountains and a bright sun – I am surrounded by peace as I gaze at my mother. Understanding the powerful influence that Peru has on its inhabitants makes me believe in this moment.

Dreams come true in Peru, and as much as I cannot fully grasp this experience, I am relaxing into what is happening rather than resisting it. Peru is an amazing place for me; it embraces me emotionally and psychologically. It has a calming effect and reminds me of soothing memories of my childhood. Even when I'm among strangers, I feel at ease, as though I have met these people before. Maybe there is a connection because we are all feeling the positive effects of being in Peru. The Sacred Valley is where I felt compelled to release any stress in my life. There is so much calmness in this place that it forces me to want the same calmness in my life. You come here unaware of its power – and then once you feel it, it becomes a part of you.

The mountains that surround me are massive compared to anything else going on in my life. Knowing that they have withstood storms but still remain grounded gives me reason to do the same. They metaphorically motivate me to let go of anything I am carrying that is making me act out of accordance with who I know I am. Accumulated stress and worry about work have always impeded my ability to focus. Focusing on past relationships hasn't allowed me to trust in the goodness of men. Analyzing past events doesn't open me up to what stands in front of me. I carry a deep worry, a fear that what I really want won't come true, a fear that maybe my dreams are too big or too hard to attain. As these thoughts surface, I look at homes built into the mountainsides, constructed many centuries ago, that are still standing. If someone could figure out how to construct something out of nothing, then how can I ever think my own dreams are unattainable? This is especially true, when I meet people who are living my dream life. When I look around and see legendary places still standing after countless years, what I thought seemed overwhelming is actually doable. The positive energy revealed throughout this land gives me hope. There are images all around showing figures of gods, outlines of birds, and beautifully sculpted animals. It is a culture rooted in respect for its land and operating out of the synchronicity of the seasons. It demonstrates the true principles of patience and sustainability.

Peru is the ideal setting for a mother-daughter conversation, because it is a place of peace after struggle. Years ago the indigenous people fought to keep their traditions, but they were met with opposition. This conflict forced native Peruvians to find ways to mask their culture within Christianity. Choosing to make peace out of conflict created a strong spirit of reconciliation. In places of spiritual power, like Peru, there are people who know how to use it and others who seek to understand.

The people of Peru feel its power and others are drawn here. Tourists come to start their own pilgrimage to peace. To stand in their own power and manifest inner qualities outwardly expressed throughout the country. They come here for courage, clarity, compassion, forgiveness, healing, peace, and strength. I initially came here for vacation hoping to recharge my battery, connect with nature and to spend time with my mother. Now that I know of the influence that it has on its visitors I am hoping to reconnect with my innocence – and to let go of anything standing in the way of my ability to believe in the supernatural. A trip to Peru is beneficial for those moving forward on the path of Ascension, going past the collective past of what is, and transforming into what we all wish to have – awakened Consciousness. Opening doors and opportunities that were not ready or visible before.

The power of this magical place, combined with my prayers, has created this special time for us to meet. I am surprised by my mother's approachability. I am initially shocked, because logically this does not seem to be real. That feeling quickly changes and I am left intrigued and curious. I feel that mom showing up as her younger self is like a genie, ready to grant my wishes. I feel she is here to address my questions – and to help me change.

The timing of this conversation is perfect. I have made some significant changes over the last few years, but I still feel as if there is something missing. Because I wasn't happy where my life was heading, I chose to shift my priorities. I created more balance at work to consciously create more time for things that were important to me. I fostered friendships based on mutual interests, and didn't box myself into maintaining ones based on years I've known a person. I reevaluated romantic interests, discontinuing relationships with men I didn't have a future with or who were not good for me. With more time to focus, I began exploring the things that interested me. I have gone to numerous self-help workshops, retreats, spiritual seminars and counseling. I have worked hard to confront and conquer my inner demons of insecurity, procrastination, and rejection.

Though I have made many improvements in my life, I still have my good days and bad days. I feel that my "younger" mom is here to give me a second chance to learn things that I initially ignored. I think she is here because she knows that I need something that cannot be learned at a seminar or in a book. She knows that I require a nurturing, honest, relatable conversation with someone who knows me, because she created me. It has been said that moms know best, and daughters know that to be true even if it's hard to admit. The best lessons are not the ones expressed when scolding. The best lessons happen when you are in the midst of a situation, and someone reaches out to you with compassion, and ways they improved their life. They are not the ones intentionally taught, but humbly felt when a person in trouble is comforted by a person who recognizes the pain as their own.

The Meeting

Since my mother looks so different, I pull out my mirror to look at myself – and notice that I, too, look just like my high school graduation picture. Black shirt, pearls, gold post earrings, curly long hair, red lipstick with my signature big dimples. My transformation is less obvious since I have not aged much since high school; the biggest change is with my hair since I recently cut off my locks for a more tapered look. After staring at her and examining myself I realize that we both are frozen at the same point in our lives. As I take another look at our faces, I notice that we are the same age.

Me to Mom: "Hi."

I greet my mother even though I am struggling to deal with my confusion and the genuineness of this moment. I feel like I need to say something to break the silence in order to put myself at ease. Even though I am nervous and unsure of her response, I ask, "Why do you think we are here?"

Mom to Me: "I don't know."

Mothers Reflection: As the words leave my mouth, I am also finding it hard to adjust to my form. I look down and see my smaller hips and thighs, and I wonder how my body could regress while my memory still remains intact. I still possess all the memories I've collected over these past thirty years as a wife, mother, and executive – but without the regrets. For once in a very long time, I am relaxed. As I look at my outfit I remember all of the dreams I had when I used to wear this – and how carefree I felt. When life decisions were more about what to wear than how to put food on the table. Mothers are supposed to know everything, but I don't know why my daughter and I are in the mountaintops of Peru in an altered dimension. Instead of acting like I have it all together, I am fine with not knowing now – but curious to find out.

Mom to Me: "I don't think it is weird for me to come back to you at this point in my life – I showed up in the way you wanted to see me. It's your dream, and just as in life, you control the experiences and how they come to you. I think we are here alone because you need my full attention; I am younger because you need a friend you can fully relate to, more than someone to guide you. You need to see me in a different form to feel my innocence, my femininity and my vulnerability. You need to see yourself in me. Since for your whole life I have been a wife and mother, you struggle with being fully able to relate to my experience and trusting my wisdom."

"When I asked you to come with me on this trip; I asked you because I enjoy your company, your humor and your spirit. This trip is hopefully the start of a different phase of our relationship, where we can do more things together as friends – and in which you will see the fullness of what our relationship can be."

As I say these words to my daughter, I begin to relax in the moment. I stop wondering, stop thinking and stop trying to figure out why we are having this experience. I let my heart guide my words, and not my head.

Me to Mom: "We look alike!"

Daughter's Reflection: As I say these words, I realize that my mother and I have a lot of similarities. Physically we both have high cheekbones, and we have the same pear-shaped build. I've never noticed how expressive her eyes are, but all my life, I have always heard that my face gives away my feelings: one look at me, and people can tell if I am happy, sad, upset or pensive. As I look into mom's eyes, I don't see the

45

scowl that I saw growing up, but instead I see a much softer face. A look of curiosity, as though she is focused only on me, and my well-being. This is important to me, because I have always felt that she was trying to balance the world on her shoulders. Although I was a top priority for her, I felt that my interests and needs were always being juggled with the other things on her plate. For the first time ever, I feel I have her undivided attention, and that I am the most important thing in her world right now. I am in competition with no one and nothing. I am in the spotlight, and I am not shying away from the light. Being a middle child, I always had to share my time/food/interests/ with someone else. I don't resent my siblings, but I've always felt that it's never been my time to shine. I don't want to waste this experience. I am full of excitement as I think about what we may talk about– just like a kid who is waiting to open presents up on Christmas morning. My excitement quickly shifts to an inquisitive nature, and just as a child who is learning how to talk asks "why" about everything. I feel as though I have regressed back to the wonder stage of development, where everything looks shiny and new – and where I want to know everything.

Sometimes when I ask a question, I have doubt in the back of my mind that the response I will receive is truthful. I respectfully listen to the answer, but I wonder if the response will be applicable to my situation. My conversation with "young mom" is different, because I have a strong feeling that she is speaking from her heart. She has proved throughout her life to be wiser than her years. I know that she knows what I need, and that is why she is here.

Mother's Reflection: As she looks at me, I have so many thoughts running through my mind of what I need to tell her. My focus goes to what I will say and how I will deliver the messages. When I pause, I see and sense my daughter's uncertainty. Seeing the emotion on her face was enough for me to get out of my head, and zero in on what she may be feeling. Since my daughter came from me, I have the ability to read her emotions as if they are my own, when I allow her to be my main focus. I think that is why I am here. As I realize that, I reach over and touch her hand so that she feels reassured. And I say something to her that I have wished someone would say to me in times of uncertainty.

Mom to Me: "I love you just the way you are. I am here with you and everything will be okay. You are exactly where you need to be. I am here to remind you how special you are, and to give you advice that will help you – things I know you may be aware of, but just need to hear again."

Daughter's Reflection: My mother's words comfort me and even though I can't explain why they feel different to me now, I accept them as truth.

Mother's Reflection: When planning the trip to Peru, we didn't know what would come from spending time apart from our normal routines. Now that we have both found each other at a different point in time we don't know what to do. We both are analytical, studying the rules before embarking on any task, but in this dream state, there are no known expectations or promised outcomes. We have found ourselves together, with full emotions in our hearts. It seems that the change in time has softened our perception of one another. Are we here because of our imagination? Are we here because of a conversation that needs to happen? Are we here because silently we have wished to share a spiritual experience together, because we relate on the deepest of levels? Are we here because in our lives we have both had a similar dream, and thanks to the magic of the Sacred Valley, has this dream now come true?

Before mom says a word, I see deep emotions in her eyes. Feeling a deep connection, and trusting her immensely, I walk over to her – and without asking, I lay my head in her lap.

Mother's Reflection: As I look at my daughter, I try to put myself in her shoes and try to process how this experience is impacting her. I asked her to come to Peru because I really enjoy her company and think she is an amazing person. Of all of my children, she "gets" me, and I am here to fully "get" her. She has always been my twin. I shouldn't be surprised by our similarities – but each time she does something that I have done, or am capable of doing, it forces me to pause and take note. I, like every mother, have always wanted to do right by my daughter. Giving her opportunities and fulfilling her dreams as I also realize parts of my life that I didn't have a chance to do when I was younger. I have always wanted to be a good mother – but this present reality, with both of us showing up at the same point in our lives, makes me wonder what prompted this experience. I want my daughter to walk away from this experience content and full of answers. To see her happy, and able to live a full life, will complete me as a mother. I hope reversing time can save my daughter from future heartache and remind her of the lessons I taught her when she was growing up. I will gladly change myself to be what she needs me to be. I am willing to do anything for her happiness. I think every mother morphs and changes depending on her child's need – a trait that is developed during pregnancy.

I want to remain focused in this moment, so that I can take in each word and emotion. Prior to coming here, I watched a movie that talked about how things develop in different dimensions of time. Contrary to popular belief, I don't think that anything is ever lost – and can be found when we are ready. We have a temporary state of forgetfulness when we allow ourselves to drift away from our center. I won't allow this experience to drift away from me. I have chosen to stay present, grounded in the knowledge that I am the creator and orchestrator of all things in my life, which includes having this dream with my daughter in Peru.

I know that inspirations can come in various forms, and the concept of time is as fluid as our perceptions. Old memories are relived when we go back to revisit them. We leave our present place when we gaze into the future, hoping for new things, and daydream about what we hope will happen. Time, and our perspective of time, both change as we develop. I truly believe that the reality we see starts earlier than the projected images. Sight, just like time, is a product of our thoughts, beliefs and actions. To travel in time is as easy as closing our eyes and dreaming. We jumped into each other's dreams at the same point in our lives, because we stand together, in solidarity of what we both want. This is a cherished time, an authentic time, an honorable time of blessed engagement, one without filters or pre-stated roles.

To show up at the exact point in each of our lives implies that we are connected. Twin existences rather than the cause and effect relationships that mothers and daughters most often have. I choose, for once in my life, to act out of impulse, moving forward knowing that this is real – even if I can't explain it. This is a time to reestablish and reconnect with what has been lost or never received – a time to stand and believe in all things. The mother and daughter connection is the epitome of all relationships because of the similarities that exist between parent and offspring; inheriting much more than looks, adopting behaviors transmitted from generation to generation.

Mothers are charged with breathing life into their children before they are able to breathe on their own. Even though my daughter can breathe on her own, I want to fill her spirit. As I sit here and look at my child, I don't just want her to survive, but thrive in all aspects of life as a professional, a mate, a friend, and one day as a mother. Whatever she chooses, I want her to feel that

51

she is enough, and that her life matters in this world. I want her to see herself as excelling, and capable of doing anything. All mothers realize that they will make mistakes, but I hope the lessons I shared with her were not clouded by what was going on in my own life at the time. There are core things that every mother wants her daughter to know – and if she didn't learn them initially, I am happy that we can review them now. I am hoping that the time we are sharing has been resolved of its conflict and judgment, and that only truth prevails. I am here in a sacred place of peace, leaning on this environment to create a utopian experience. I am here to express my innermost thoughts regarding how to live a successful and loving life.

I want my daughter to be fully open with her heart, soul, mind, spirit and energy. As we sit here in the Sacred Valley, I want her to release anything holding her back. I want her to be fully healed, restored, and return to the innocent soul I birthed. Eighteen represents a time of independence for a girl becoming a woman, a point when intuition is refined and when confidence begins to find stability. Since we are both meeting at a time of naivety, we won't be distracted by the guilt of bad decisions or unmet expectations experienced in adulthood. My daughter is too special not to live her best life, and I will do whatever it takes to ensure that happens. As we both revisit this time, I am forced to think about everything that has helped me in my life, and package it in a way for her to receive it. I am thinking through all the important things that a strong woman needs to know. Things I have gained in my life, things passed down to me from my elders and those things I know to be true. These can transform and strengthen a woman's life. I believe we have been granted this dream to bring us closer to what we seek, a bonded relationship grounded in honesty, truth, love and understanding. Since I am the mother, I will make the first move.

<u>Self-Love</u>

Mom to Me: "Do you love yourself"

Me to Mom: "I don't know how to answer that question." The right answer is "yes," but when I think of how I have treated myself and allowed others to treat me, I don't know if I really love myself. When I was growing up, love was shown by sacrifice. I was constantly reminded of how my life altered the lives of others, and that since I was loved, others chose to do things for me. I often felt like a burden, more than a blessing.

Me to Mom: "How do you know you love yourself?"

Mom to Me: "When you listen to what you want, and go after it. When you are gentle with yourself and when you don't give up on yourself even if you make a mistake. When you see potential in yourself, and continue to try even when all you experience is failure. Love is endless possibilities that you see, even when others only see your mistakes. Love is knowing that you have value – and remaining open to opportunities until you see your value. Love is evident when you are around a young child. No matter how many times a baby falls, throws its rattle or has an accident, someone is there to help the baby because everyone believes the baby will learn and do better. Women must constantly see that growing baby inside of them, and keep nurturing the love until what they know to be true becomes a reality."

"You know you love yourself when you confidently listen to yourself and trust yourself to make decisions. When you feel confident to speak up and express your thoughts. When you can stand up for yourself, even when your popularity is challenged. When you are not afraid to take risks because you believe in your ability to achieve. You know you love yourself when you experience a setback but find the courage to start again. When you experience rejection but remain open to try new experiences. Rejection can lead to self-love if you learn to turn within rather than seeking external validation. When you don't allow other people's disappointment to cloud your opinion of yourself, and when you can see the goodness inside you every day. When you stay committed to your journey without being distracted by others – or comparing yourself to people who may look like they have more."

"The most important thing that a woman must know is love of self. I wish I had spent more time on loving myself than on changing so I would get love from others. I gave other people numerous chances, even after they messed me over, but I was always more critical of myself even if I made the smallest mistake. Trust is earned – love is not. Love is an inner belief that people are good, and it's a commitment to assist with growing that goodness. It is easy to think you have self-love if you receive compliments, have a good job or flashy possessions. Love is often confused with what is attractive, but it is much deeper. Looks can be deceiving because trends change over time, whereas love evolves over time. It's an appreciation of your personality – the things that make you great, and the motivation to work on other parts of yourself."

"It's an unconditional love in which you continue to give yourself what you need. If you need food, you eat; if you need good health, you make changes; if you need love, you find soul-filling love; and if you need a break, you rest. You do things because there is a need – without consideration of what you feel you deserve or have earned. Unconditional love of self is the precursor to one's ability to love another. Love is more about connecting with another to fill a need and less about empty action. To love, you must know love. My first introduction to real love was God. I began to see God as my friend during daily interactions of devotion and expressions of my needs. The more I prayed, the more I saw things changing in my life for the better. I started to believe that I was worthy of blessings. My relationship with God made me see myself as having power. As I learned to trust and believe in God, I began to believe in myself, which cultivated and established self-love. God is love – and finally I see a love within myself."

"We are in the Sacred Valley in Peru, and I have found more peace here than anywhere in my life. Women must relax in order to restore our energy. We tend to be constant givers, and we will easily lose focus and perspective if we don't take time to replenish. Love of self makes you realize that you are important enough to be cherished – everything else you need is built on the foundation of self-love."

<u>Curiosity</u>

Mom to Me: "Why did you agree to come with me to Peru?"

Me to Mom: "I don't know, you asked and I thought it would be fun."

Mom to Me: "Is that all? Was there anything else that motivated you to come? You have never been here; were you interested in seeing the country?"

Me to Mom: "Mom, you are the world traveler. I didn't even Google Peru – I trusted that you were making a good choice with your decision to come to Peru. Since I trust you, I didn't really look to see what Peru had to offer. I guess I was most curious to see how we could handle being together for two weeks."

Mom to Me: "You have jokes, but its sounds like curiosity was a part of your decision process?"

Me to Mom: "Yes, I guess you are right, curiosity was a factor."

Mom to Me: "The most important thing a woman can do is tap into her inner sense of curiosity. There is a place within that lightens up, and wakes up, when an external interest matches an emotional feeling. When that happens, there is a strong response that wakes us up and energizes us to inquire and gravitate to the source of the curiosity. A feeling that keeps us engaged and is not restricted by money or any other limitation. The type of curiosity that encourages dialogue and researches for answers. The type of thinking that leads the mind to question, and the body to take action. The questions are usually more telling than the answers that you may find, because the questions give clues to one's mindset, which implicitly demonstrates who we are."

"College is all about curiosity – from selecting where you will go, to identifying a degree and developing friendships. When you think you have all the answers, without asking yourself why you have the curiosity to do something, you are limiting your ability to pursue critical parts of your life. That's a mistake that *my* mom cautions me about making. It's a mistake that is common with women, especially for women who concentrate more on being accepted by others than on awakening the power within. Many times, women replace curiosity with companionship, thinking that by pursing their object of affection, they can quiet the constant questions of their heart. Curiosity is not only about answering those questions, but it is also about accepting the journey that comes along with answering those questions. With curiosity you need freedom, freedom to explore and freedom to quench the thirst of curiosity. Women need something that sparks their interest, and invigorates the type of energy that sustains attentiveness and dedication. Life is about curiosity – and about creating experiences that satisfy that curiosity. Although people, especially mothers, think that their curiosity can be solely fulfilled by their families, it is a deeper calling – one not limited by bloodline, and one that is meant to impact many."

"Everyone thinks that college is the answer to every question and the only way to create a successful, happy, and balanced life. Instead of college being the destination, it is only the start of the journey. It's a journey of asking yourself what you enjoy. A journey of dedication and focused commitment until graduation. Often it is not about what your major is, in college, but the type of experiences you face, that makes college so meaningful. It is a microcosm of the real world, where you are forced to interact and engage with new people – people of different backgrounds and beliefs. A fixed amount of time meant to expedite the learning process and personal development. An opportunity to prove yourself and show others your character. College is a time of growth as you are exposed to new experiences and uncover new things about yourself."

"You must love yourself enough to follow your curiosity. Often, people have great ideas but degrade themselves so much that they never choose to pursue them. They don't think that they are strong enough to finish what they start, or that the idea is good enough for others to see its value. The confidence to pursue your curiosity builds on the belief that your thoughts are good enough to follow. Without this confidence, you will never build your competence."

Daughter's Reflection: With the advice that my mother has given me related to curiosity, I follow my inquisitiveness and ask her questions about dreams. Before I speak, I pause for a second since it seems ironic that I would ask about dreams while in a dream.

Dreams

Me to Mom: "How do you know if a dream is important enough for you to go after and what things should you consider before you spend your time and resources?"

Mom to Me: "Curiosity is what happens when you are awake and conscious of your actions, when you pursue interests with purpose. Dreams however are born from a subconscious place, the part of your spirit where your authentic self lives. Adults sometimes stop dreaming because dreams can't be controlled, and the act of dreaming is the act of surrendering to one's imagination – which can be scary. When you listen to the inspiration that exists within you, the source of your imagination is deeper than the present. It is not created by logic, but materialized by the foundation of life – something more powerful than reality. For logical people it is easy to close off their dream state, since dreams often don't make sense; especially if the dreams don't fit easily into their life. Dreams require investment, and if there is not a proven immediate return on that investment of time and money, many people lose patience and walk away from the process."

"Don't be solely focused on the financial aspects of what it will take to develop a dream. Do not choose to ignore a dream because of the amount of time you think it will take, or the things that you feel you will miss out on by pursing your dream. Focus rather on the dream, and why you think this dream has been given to you, and what it will provide to you in your life. You exercise patience when you choose to concentrate more on the process then the dream. Often times the lessons learned are more rewarding then the dream itself. Don't let doubt creep into your dream space – and when you find yourself feeling doubtful, write down your fears. As you write down your fears also write down one thing that will make that fear not come true. If you can envision positive outcomes, you will improve your mindset. The more you focus on how you are the exception to the rules, the more you become that exception. Dreams are not meant to confine you or constrict your ability to imagine; they are meant to unleash your every thought. Faith allows your mind to believe in your hopes and desires. Don't fear what has not happened; don't run from what you have not faced. Surrender and submit to the experience and leave your ego behind. Any emptiness or insecurities around what failed belongs in the past."

"Even when you are not ready or don't work directly towards fulfilling your dream, keep the curiosity around your dreams alive. There are many musicians who chose to major in business so they would have a way to support themselves while they pursued their dreams on the side. As long as there is energy around dreams, the dream does not die. As you devote more time to dreams, more opportunities present themselves that make you realize that your dreams are closer than you think. Even when you don't work full time towards a goal, all the energy, beliefs and thoughts surrounding the dream are not lost if they work towards its creation. Time is an illusion. If you have curiosity and passion, these feelings never die, but show up in other ways; they pull at you until that dream materializes. When a dream is strong enough, nothing can stop it. When money is a concern, it may delay the realization of the dream – but nothing can stop a dream from coming true. Free will, persistence and a deep desire will always outpace financial limitations. In a blink of an eye, a dream can be over – so when the opportunity presents itself, try to clear your mind and heart so that your whole being can be submerged and you can experience it fully."

Daughter's Reflection: I understand what mom is saying, and I get her perspective on dreaming. For me, every time I have a dream, it comes with subsequent inspired actions that lead me on a road to discovery. For me, every dream came with a journey where I learned more about myself; which has held true with the dream I am having right now.

__Journey__

Me to Mom: "What is a journey, and what do I need to have on my journey?"

Mom to Me: "A journey is what you learn over the course of an experience. Journeys often change and have no set course; the prerequisite for a journey is a willingness to remain open. Journeys are not always about new places: sometimes they involve revisiting what you already know, or returning back home. The end destination does not define the journey, only the emotions and feelings conjured up along the way. The best journeys are the ones that move freely and build momentum throughout. Those are the ones with life-changing experiences; situations that occur that allow you to appreciate things differently. A journey is not only the planned path you take, but what you feel when going along your charted course. The path you choose creates the memories that are generated; you can either stick with your usual routine or try something new. New opportunities are the ones that are presented when you have no comfort level or no prior knowledge to fall back on. Life is a reflector: it projects back to you the areas you focus on. If your thoughts are based on old experiences, you will get more of the same. If those experiences were not things that you want to revisit, then you must ask yourself what you want, and actively change your attention to those things. The complexity of change is that it's new; you have no knowledge of what to do – so you have to rely on curiosity and instincts more than proven experiences. You can speak things into existence if what you want mirrors how you feel at your deepest level. You can't expect miracles to happen when you still carry a lot of guilt or unfinished business from your past. The miracle of manifesting is when you believe you can have what you want regardless of your past. The work isn't proving you deserve it but undoing anything that says you can't. The interesting thing about an emotional journey is that it is one trip where you need to let go of baggage in order to move forward. Fresh experiences and being open to try different things will cause a resurgence of energy. The type of drive that is needed to progress."

"When differences show up in how you think your journey will unfold, you may question why things are happening as you work to figure out how to respond to the change. Uncertainty, worrying about the unknown, and seeking understanding are all normal reactions.

Without answers, feelings of insecurity often set in, and instead of seeing the opportunities that exist, we label these differences as obstacles – things placed in our way to stop us from reaching our destination. Often, feelings of inadequacy then follow as we ask ourselves the question of "why am I here" – a question not specifically related to our present situation, but the bigger question of our existence. The journey of life is one where we don't know everything, nor could we ever predict everything we will face. The key to navigating the journey of life is to know ourselves in a way where we learn how to tap into unused or underutilized resources within – almost in the way we exercise and train muscles."

"When we are born we are given free will. We are given the power to decide what we want. When used, free will builds determination and discernment. As we condition our senses to be more aware of our wants, we better understand how to navigate life. Once you know your motivation, or what triggers personal resistance, don't fight the information you have. Very often, instead of accepting and using this information, you criticize yourself for what you lack rather than identifying the things that make you strong. Strength comes from usage: when you work something, it builds over time and you see progress. If you want to be a stronger person, you will need to stretch your emotional muscles by pushing past your comfort zone. Don't force results – but follow your intuition by taking action. If you like someone, call them first and take the first step to tell them how you feel. Be the first to say sorry if you need to apologize. If there is tension in one of your relationships, reach out to the person and state the obvious. You grow the most when you show up to give more than you receive in order to grasp the full experience."

"There is a delicate line between stressing and stretching. Stress implies that you force yourself to do things with little regard for how you are feeling. Stretching works within your boundaries. It acknowledges that you are going beyond what's comfortable while respecting your body. It leverages your foundation so that you are able to build strength and improve flexibility. If we listen to our bodies and move at our own speed, we learn things in our own time and get what we need out of the journey. The ability to sustain throughout the journey is its own reward. Successful people don't always get things right or have the code to happiness. They do however make a decision to keep moving regardless of what they face. It's not that they have all the answers, but they have learned to control their fear so it doesn't paralyze their progress. Instead of giving it the power to stop them, they choose to channel that energy to motivate them. Pathways we face in life are really just journeys into our soul. If you want to face anything with hope and certainty, the first thing you must do is deal with the emotional rollercoaster that is within."

"A journey is an opportunity to blossom, and when fully engaged, it creates an ability to see things that were once missing from your life. Just like a GPS, your mind saves all your journeys. You remember the route that you took, as well as all the turns and storms you endured. The way you go is never the way you return – and that is the beauty of life. That is why it is so important to be aware, so we don't miss out on important lessons. The miracle of life is that even when you get lost, you have an innate ability to find your way back home – and what you may have missed going one way, you always have another opportunity to claim upon your return."

Focus

Me to Mom: "I understand the importance of a journey, and I see that there could be many different journeys in one's life. You also mentioned distractions, which makes me think about focus. How do you stay focused on the things that matter most, when you are pulled in different directions? For me, I have multiple dreams – and sometimes it seems my dreams don't always work together and support a bigger plan. With so many things I want to do, how do I figure out what should take precedence?"

Mom to Me: "There will always be something that grabs your attention. Always be someone that you are drawn to help and there will always be something that pulls at your heart and demands your time. You have to decide what is important for you to do, and what you should allow others to do for themselves. As women, we tend to be people pleasers – thinking that if something is to be done correctly, we have to be the one to do it. Women create inflated personas so that we can justify our worth and feel needed. We develop the illusion that if we love someone we need to be heavily involved their life. We often invite ourselves into situations so that others rely on us and we feel valued. We often get weary – not from productive work, but from emotionally exerting ourselves in places that were not designed for us. When we train ourselves to be everything for everybody, we respond to any request for help as if it is an emergency. Creating that fight-or-flight response to everything in life wears down your spirit. Not everything is a twelve-alarm fire, and when things don't go as you planned, it is not time for you to panic or worry. When we make everything urgent, we clutter our ability to respond appropriately to what surrounds us. Clutter, chaos and drama make it hard to see what really matters. Distractions serve only one purpose, and that is to take us away from our focus – those important things that make us whole."

"There is a fear that the journey you take by following your curiosity will not be worth it. What if the ending does not justify the course you have taken? What if you feel that the investment you made was wasted? What if you don't receive what you worked hard to get? When thoughts like that come up – and trust me, they will – you have to stop. You have chosen a path and if you need to change, change but don't wallow in regrets. Regrets rob you of your ability to trust yourself and your joy."

Daughter's Perspective: For me, my ability to focus was only related to those areas of life where I had the assurance that I could accomplish the task at hand. If there was any doubt, I would focus more on what could go wrong than on the task at hand. This mindset made me obsessed with the "what if's," since in my mind I needed to think through all possibilities. My focus has always been on winning. I felt I had to win, and my thought pattern limited what I allowed myself to engage in and try. In relationships, I fixated all of my energy on one person, thinking it was all or nothing. If it didn't work, I blamed myself and then withdrew from others. I wouldn't focus on experiences long enough to be grateful for what I had. It's easy to lose perspective in the pursuit, especially if you are not grounded in what is important. What I emphasize magnifies, spending time on what could go wrong made me see errors first even if there were opportunities to make them better. I now see that things failed not because they were destined to fail but because I was holding back.

Me to Mom: "Mom, I usually feel distracted when I am just about to reach a platform of success, like right before graduation or before a major change. It comes when something good is about to happen in my life. I know something big is going to happen when I start envisioning success, but then right afterward I have cold feet. It's as though I feel I am on the cusp of something big, and I fear how I am going to handle the change. Since I struggle with how to adjust, or if I will really achieve what I want, I prepare myself for disappointment, just in case I don't get it. It's as if I am ready for it because of how hard I have worked, but at the same time I am not emotionally prepared if I don't get it. I guess I spend more time doing the tangible work and not enough time dealing with my headspace. Since I have made a pattern of going after things that I am not passionate about, I have grown accustomed to feelings of complacency. It's hard to get excited when I know I am lukewarm about something. Even when I am really curious about something, I often choose to settle for what I know I can achieve. Finding confidence in my known skills and accomplishments versus venturing out to try something exciting. Since I have grown accustomed to average living, I have learned to control my emotions. I constantly create contingency plans since my heart has not been in many of my actions. It's easy to prepare for disappointment when you forget how good it feels to get something you really want. Instead of focusing on my desires, I have chosen to allow distractions to clutter my perspective."

Mom to Me: "Whenever you go after something big, there is the initial work needed to achieve it. Then there is the emotional growth you must endure to feel worthy enough to embrace it once it shows up. If you just focus on the work, you won't be able to see the blessing when it shows up. If you only focus on the emotions, you won't be able to keep what you receive."

"Focus streamlines goals and dreams, which is the energy you have to rely on to carry you when doubt shows up along the journey. Focus doesn't mean that everything will turn out well, but it will at least allow you to be aware of what you need to see. Allowing you the intuitive ability to change directions and modify things if need be. Life is not about setting a course and sticking to it; it is about allowing yourself to adapt to things and see opportunities that once were hidden. As your exposure increases, your experiences enrich. If you only stick to one way of thinking, you won't see life's three-dimensional picture – one part truth, one part observation, and one part perception. How we perceive things dominates all other views because it is our interpretation of things based on our outlook. Your feelings drive your perception of what you see. To fully understand them focus on what you want, rather than what others tell you is important. Focus on being honest even if it means you may disappoint others. Ultimately, focus on your full happiness, and maintain a healthy outlook. Selfishness is when you only think about yourself without consideration of others. Sustainability is when you know that the time you spend on yourself will impact everyone for the better – yourself included. Focus on sustainability!"

"Also, don't be afraid of distractions. They will come. Distraction feels like doubt but it can also be a healthy diversion. It forces you to stop doing what you thought was important to assess if the new request for you time is more important. It can cause us to press pause if our interest can wait to be pursued. Or we may recommit ourselves with renewed fervor if the interest aligns to a greater purpose. When you face any choice, keep an open mind and have the courage to change directions without the need to justify. Have the confidence to pursue other interests without guilt and the strength to invest your all – because you are fully committed to being your best. The best way to safeguard damaging distractions is not to ignore them, as if they don't exist, but to realize that they will come with every pursuit you have. Distractions are a part of the human psyche: a clever way to weed out dreamers from doers. It's meant to either build greater inner resolve or to create constant restrictive barriers. When used the right way, distractions reestablish interests, planting our roots even stronger so that the next time we are met with distraction, we don't waver. If we use distraction to train our perseverance, we get wiser as we get older. If we use distraction to create anxiety and choose to worry, we place unnecessary weight on situations. Sometimes things fall apart – not because they were not intended to succeed but because the additional weight burdened what was intended to be light."

"Some distractions are self-imposed, a fabricated way to identify a good excuse if you are afraid that you won't succeed. Something to fall back on and tell others when they keep you accountable for things you've said. Achievement is what everyone wants, but it is also scary if you are someone who has struggled to receive it. I believe that the number of support groups has increased so that there is a place for people to go to commiserate about things when they don't work out. In my opinion, it is the same reason why there has been an uptick in life coaches: people are looking for an outlet. We all need help, to feel supported, and to hear that everything will be okay. Who better to encourage us than someone who has stood in our shoes? No one wants to be alone. Focus is hard when you have distractions, but focus can be easier when you are working together with others to achieve a common goal."

Impact

Me to Mom: "You reference common goals when working with others and impact. How do you define impact?"

Mom to Me: "We all want to be remembered and feel like our life mattered. What gives us life is our ability to have an impact. Impact: the ability to touch others, leave a positive impression, and influence those around us. We are impacted by our surroundings and who we let into our lives. The seeds planted by others set actions in motion, sometimes without our knowledge. Seeds that establish roots and shape our disposition. Our mood precedes our physical presence and has a direct effect on all relationships."

"Impact has become the universal form of judgment: a way to assess the magnitude or value of one's life. It is the one thing we chase, because if our impact is great, we feel we are great. Impact is what we all want, but don't know how to achieve. Once we have a sense of impact, we often become addicted to the feeling of creation. Searching not for the feeling of impact, but needing to qualify the magnitude of impact. When you are preoccupied with numbers and have a need to validate everything, you lose sight of the true purpose of impact. It's the children you mentored that go on to lead balanced lives. It is the number of people who feel better for being in your presence though they don't know why. Sometimes the simple things you do create the largest impact – such as when you see someone as good, important and valuable. We associate impact with action, often expecting achievement. Impact comes with the pressure to maintain high standards."

"Impact is a very interesting concept, not because of what it means, but because of how we expect impact to look. Our expectations of race, gender, age, and physical ability shape our assumptions around talents. It is a damaging stigma that we have created based on appearances. I am telling you this because people may expect less of you based on your gender, race and age. I felt it growing up so I don't want you to be surprised if you have the same realization. I dealt with this by trying to prove people wrong and pushing myself in everything I did. I over-performed so people saw me as important and treated me like I was irreplaceable. Impact can be your greatest motivator or your greatest stressor. It is our greatest asset as a community, when we combine our efforts and impact each other in a positive way. But if you can't live up to the pressure, you can feel like a failure. Don't let the drive to leave an impact force you into decisions or plans that are not yours. Don't let impact make you afraid to try because you are afraid to fail."

"The desires of your heart are the greatest indicators of where you will leave an impact. Love is also the greatest predicator, because if you love something you will enjoy doing it and become good at it. When you see how your efforts impact others, you will have a greater appreciation for your gifts. Sometimes you see immediate benefit and others times it won't be as direct; but don't get discouraged. To see yourself as impactful without having to evaluate every action will set you free. You will go far in life and with each experience you will touch many people. Some of whom will never have the opportunity to say thank you, others you will never know their name."

Me to Mom: "What is the greatest level of impact?"

Mom to Me: "Love and authentically connecting with others motivates our spirit in the greatest way. The foundation of impact is love. We do what we do hoping that when we connect with others, together we can do more and recover what we think we have lost. True connections will make you come alive and erase any pain from your past. The greatest impact on your life is when you are doing what you love with the people you love. There is a magic that is created when people come together for a common goal. Intangible things that we can't explain that cause miracles to happen every day."

"I believe that the more we believe in miracles, the more we see miracles; which are the compounded effect of impact. Miracles are when the goodness of life is multiplied into more love and blessings, when small efforts create larger impact. Prayer, charity, giving people a second chance all create greater impact and believing in and seeing the good in ourselves and others creates the utmost impact. People who continue to believe, in spite of their actions and what others have done to them have the greatest impact in life. God knows we have flaws; he made us. In spite of the perfection that we portray, our flaws connect us with others. Our ability to overcome these things creates optimism in the world, for others to follow our lead and move forward too. Life is better when your focus is on meaningful impact. It is better when you have awareness of the ways you impact others, and you work to make sure they are positive. Impulse can sometimes be confused with impact. With impulse you act without hesitation; often with no clear direction. Whereas impact means you are grounded, achieving a level of balance before acting. Influence touches our core, inspiration moves us to act – and impact is the result of both."

Me to Mom: "What are the effects of impact?"

Mom to Me: "If you are blessed, you will see the positive effects of your life and they will show up as joy, happiness, accomplishment and appreciation. Joy requires a level of maturity to know the difference between temporary happiness and longstanding bliss. It also involves tenacity, so that you stay committed to see things through to the end. It's achieved only when you fully embrace reality, and allow your true emotions to come through. Tenacity means that you stay in a place of observation long enough to experience the feelings and lessons. Happiness is a different type of sensation than joy; it is a component of joy, but doesn't have the full intensity. We break life into years, months, weeks, hours and minutes; looking at happiness in the same way. Happiness tends to describe a season, whereas joy is defined over an extended period of time. Happiness gives joy the momentum to continue. The joy and happiness you feel is how your spirit interacts with others. People are drawn to positive energy. Positive people tend to accomplish more because others want to work with them. The tenacity of staying committed to joy allows them not to be short sided. They don't allow setbacks to impact their long term vision. They believe they are meant for greatness and hold onto that belief."

"Accomplishments result in desired outcome, a hope that what we achieve will bring us a self of fulfillment. The definition of being open is the process of surrendering to an experience wholeheartedly; not knowing what will happen or come to you. Accomplishment serves as a starting point that all goals build upon. In times of doubt, people often revert back to the things said about them to give them a starting point of where to build from. When you are young and you hear "good job," it gives power to an insecure part of yourself – and from that place you now have assurance that maybe you can do other things right. There has to be one person who sees your importance. And, hopefully, you thought that person was me. I have *always* seen your value. However ultimately the only perspective that matters is how you see yourself. True accomplishment is when you can motivate yourself regardless of whether others see what you see or believe what you believe."

Disappointment, Mistakes, and Judgment

Mom to Me: "Often times, on the road to accomplishment, you deal with disappointment. The good news is the resilience of the human spirit allows us to overcome hurt. I raised you to be strong and gave you everything my mother, father, aunt, uncles, teachers and church family gave me. You come from a very strong and wise family; we are survivors. So regardless of what you may feel about yourself there is power in your name."

"Disappointment is an emotion you must learn to overcome. It's damaging because it stops you from trying once you hit a roadblock. The pain subsides over time, but the impact that it has on your psyche can make you so protective that you don't want to take any risks at all for fear of being hurt again. The fear of pain paralyzes your ability to move forward. Disappointment impacts all of us, and no one likes to experience it, but it is a universal rite of passage – something that, when properly dealt with, loses its sting. Disappointment, like all other lower emotions, can only take root when you believe it to be true; when you see yourself as the disappointment rather than seeing a disappointment as an external challenge."

"Chronic disappointment or depression happens when you accept this emotion as being a part of your life, rather than acknowledging the strength that you possess inside to overcome whatever you face. Anxiety just like fear becomes a looming feeling. It possesses no immediate threat but creates distress when you consistently give it power. When you feel and think that disappointment will be a part of every experience, even before new things start, your mind is programmed to expect failure. When you accept disappointment, it becomes normal to you. Disappointment is one of those things you cannot pinpoint, or even remember your first encounter. If the emotion happens frequently, you begin to expect it even before something happens."

"The devastating effects of disappointment are not always what is done to us, but have more to do with how we deal with the letdown and what happens within our inner spirit. If you accept this experience as an indication of what your life will be, you create a defeatist mentality and you will see yourself as a victim. If you use this emotion to wake you up to what you need to do, you give yourself options. When a relationship does not work, instead of thinking about what you have lost, think about how you can intensify the loving relationships that you *do* have. Write down the things that made you happy in the relationship and seek to keep those things in the next. Appreciate what you experienced and be grateful that you now know what you need in love. Think about what you can do with the extra time; is there a hobby that you have neglected that you now have the time to pursue? When you don't get a job is it really about the job or the respect you wish you had? When people you trusted let you down, instead of assuming they acted with bad intention, reach out to them to understand. When disappointment is used as a means to have greater awareness, then the pain is a signal, rather than a continuation of suffering."

Mom to Me: "What else do you want to know; what else do you feel you *should* know?"

Me to Mom: "All this advice sounds good but all my life I have felt accident prone. I feel like no matter what I do, I keep making mistakes. You said that I am going through these things in life in order to learn a lesson. If that is the case, why is so much attention given to mistakes?"

Mom to Me: "A mistake is a term used when we don't know or can't explain why our expectations are not met. We call it a mistake because on some level we believe it is our fault, that we created this "wrongdoing." But if we believed or reminded ourselves that everything always turns out the way it is meant to, which is well, why would we ever go through an exercise where we beat ourselves up? The bigger question is not what a mistake is; it is why people, especially women, allow mistakes to ruin their life. The mistake doesn't ruin one's life; it is the associated feeling and distraction that mistakes cause that is so damaging. We associate mistake with shame, and we lock ourselves in a spiritual prison, almost like solitary confinement. We don't let anyone in for fear of judgment and we don't leave because we don't trust ourselves. When we grow tired of the self-imposed isolation we look for distractions to make us feel better. Gravitating to anything even if it is temporary; food, people, parties, and compliments. Anything that makes us forget our pain, creating a temporary sense of security. This false state of normalcy can't be sustained, because truth always is revealed, and there will always come a time when you are forced to face the truth about yourself."

"It's temporary because what you are running from has not been dealt with, and it is waiting for you to address it. Things ignored don't shrink with time; they grow, creating a web of confusion around the core issues. And now, instead of just dealing with the initial perceived mistake, you must comb through a host of other emotions that you created by trying to run away from the mistake. Distractions take us away from what needs to be developed within. The decisions we make out of shame create an aftermath of problems. They pull us further and further away from our center. We forget our power. The easiest, yet hardest thing is standing up and seeing yourself as the creator – and the fixer – of your own life. For when you own the experience, you are then accountable for the outcome."

"When we make decisions that differ from what others would do or what is acceptable, we think we have made a mistake. It's easier for people to gravitate towards an anchored thought or a common practice than to figure things out for themselves. What is right, or what is considered right, implies that everything else is wrong, which is the starting point for judgment. We have a society of rule-followers who take pride in obedience, and rule-breakers who are not afraid of taking a risk; both seek happy lives without true understanding of what that means or how to get it."

"Judgment is a shortcut that we take when understanding, compassion and patience seem to take too much time. Judgment is what comes up when it is easier to analyze something based on what you think you know, in order to draw a quick conclusion, instead of allowing the experience to develop over time."

Me to Mom: "If mistakes are apart of development, why do people always focus on what's right and wrong. We have so many religions. It seems like each one is saying basically the same thing yet there are so many conflicts and wars. As a society why is being right so important?"

Mom to Me: "Being right gives a feeling of control and reinforces our need to feel powerful. In our ability to prove our rightness, or demonstrate our intelligence, we validate our existence. We are taught from a very young age about absolutes; stanch truths about what should and shouldn't be done. We operate in the black-and-white so much of the time that we often forget what the rationale is for these rules."

"Right people are often lonely people; they surround themselves with only their version of the truth. They are afraid to see another way or change their perspective because they don't want to be seen as wrong. People have spent their whole life on pointing out others faults to make themselves appear better. When you feel better about yourself because of what someone else did wrong, what you have is contingency happiness – which can change at any moment."

"You need to know that my happiness is tied to your happiness and your ability to live a full life. I didn't want to stifle your spirit as a child but my main focus was your safety. I had to protect you until you were able to protect yourself. I know I didn't do everything right but I got you here and that is all that matters. We have a chance to make both of our dreams come true. The only thing to do is to move forward together."

Daughters Reflection: I look up at my mom and smile and feel like all of her past mistakes have been forgotten. Any resentment or regrets are also gone.

Me to Mom: "I agree and I am ready to move forward with you Mom, but another thing that is holding me back is comparisons. I compare myself to others a lot and it makes me feel really bad about things I have not experienced or accomplished. I want to stop doing it, but whenever I feel low, that is the first thing I do. Why do we compare ourselves to others?"

Mom to Me: "One person told me that if you want to rob yourself of happiness, compare your life with someone else's journey. Comparisons take who we are, and then switch them into what we thought we should be. By forcing us to look at things and ourselves through the eyes of another person we create insecurity. When we compare ourselves to others, we assume that the obvious differences are the only things we lack. We think that if we deal with the obvious, we would have what we want, and by comparing ourselves to others, we think we have enough knowledge to build a case against ourselves. If only I was skinnier I would date more, if only I was smarter I would get that promotion, if only I had more friends I would feel supported, if only I was married I wouldn't feel lonely. People date because they are open; promoted because they have an advocate. Support is not about how many friends you have but the quality of the friendship – and loneliness is a state of mind, not a status."

"By switching out the characters we play with those that are around us, we hope to change our own outcome in life. Assuming that if we master the one thing that we believe we lack, successful love will appear immediately – as if God is holding our happiness hostage until we switch our lives with someone else. It becomes comical when we verbalize the silent beliefs of the shadows in our hearts, those things we follow but never would communicate. We play God when we think that we can control our own life by following someone else's blueprint. How can we seek to comprehend the full picture, when we only see what others allow us to see; a small snippet of a complex story?"

"A comparison of talents, strength, beauty or intelligence implies that you operate the same way as the person you have chosen to idolize. It implies that you both are similar; that the situation presented to that person would have been presented to you. It disregards the distinctive spirit of a person or the belief in destiny. Comparison is a waste of time and emotion. The scenarios you play out in your mind won't come true. Instead of getting insights about life you insult the unique spirit of your life. If you choose to blame all your failures on what you are not, you will fail to recognize the beauty of who you are. You will fail to see all the things you could have been able to do with your strengths."

Me to Mom: "So if comparisons make us critical of ourselves, why do we criticize others – and what can we do to stop?"

Mom to Me: "Criticism is a judgment; every time you criticize someone else you are really just showcasing what you hate about yourself. Criticism is not about what we criticize. It has less to do with the other person and more to do with ourselves and our own insecurities. When we criticize, we openly talk about someone else and what they are doing wrong. We would rather focus on them than turn the attention inward in order to change what we dislike about ourselves. We criticize when we are afraid that someone else will find what we are trying to hide. By placing attention on someone else's flaws, hopefully our own flaws can remain hidden. It's a classic human tactic to gossip about someone else's life so that our own issues remain quietly intact. It is not until we detach from the chaos that we can focus enough on ourselves to identify what we so critically protect from others' evaluation."

"Quiet time exposes our true self, the thing we wish to hide from others. Quiet time allows our deepest fears and thoughts to surface to the top. Things that may have been forgotten or things we were unaware of that mattered to us. Quiet time makes us ask ourselves the tough questions. Quiet time is often avoided, because it can feel pointless to sit with your thoughts without reason. We prove our worth by what we do and how we plan for the future. Quiet time makes us feel inadequate if we cannot document why we are quiet, or if we don't have a reason for the silence. Quiet time is something much different than what it represents, because our spirits are innately silent. In our quiet time, our voices and our bodies may be quiet – but our thoughts are moving. Those thoughts provide our deepest insight about how we view ourselves and the world around us. When we run from quiet time, we are really running from what will bring us the most peace. Although quiet, energy is constantly flowing. We use that energy to focus and complete what is at the top of our agenda. Without quiet time we are just aimlessly moving through life."

"When an object is propelled into the air it doesn't mean that it will meet its target. Whereas if the person in control of that object has clear direction, there is a higher chance that the object will meet its mark. We are just like those balls: without purpose, we go unguided – bumping into each other, hitting things we never meant to hit and injuring innocent bystanders. That is the thing about quiet time: it is in those times that dreams have the opportunity to find inspiration. It is in quiet time that books and movies are animated and brought to life."

"Quiet time is necessary, and it is wise to take this time to see and observe the places of your life that have been forgotten. In time, you will achieve peacefulness and clarity; things will unlock within yourself because quiet time is the gift that we give ourselves. It is a gift you also give to others, because if you are filled with more joy, you treat others with more love. Love is the greatest antidote for criticism. Quiet time allows you to sit with your words and actions; allowing you to feel their potential effects. It makes you own the feelings you project and allows you to see everything in full circle."

"Many people, especially women, fight time alone because they think it means that they are lonely, but if you don't fight it, it becomes a cherished time. It's an opportunity to clear your mind of the expectations of others, so that you can identify what you want, without obligations. When you remove distractions in life, you can figure out what you like and make decisions based on compatibility, and not just out of a need for companionship. This is when growth happens."

<u>Confusion</u>

Me to Mom: "I understand the importance of quiet time, but what happens when you find it hard to clear your mind?"

Mom to Me: "Your mind will be cluttered initially. You are used to operating out of routine so your natural tendency is to do and not be still. Quiet time is a learned behavior; you can train yourself to be still by building it into your schedule. Maybe initially you can only sit for a minute but over time that increases. Quiet time is not a race it is a dedication to doing something different and a devotion to peace. By placing an importance on peace, you change your mindset around quiet time. Over time you will achieve clarity but initially you will be confused by the flood of emotions that come up. Your goal shouldn't be to judge those feelings or rush to fix them. Learning to sit with emotions without an immediate need to react is the art of control. You are not procrastinating you are waiting for clarity."

"Confusion or the absence of clarity is what you feel when you want something – but the details surrounding it appear to be missing. It is the time delay associated with the want and receiving it. Clarity gives us the ability to connect the dots, whereas confusion only shows us a random assortment of events. The power in quiet time is that the solution you seek lies in the random assortment. Quiet time reveals what is best suited for you through the process of contemplation."

"Taking a second look is the soul's balancing act, a way to force you to examine things before moving forward. The prerequisite of conviction is contemplation; if you weigh your options and still come back to the place where you started, you can move forward with the clarity that you seek. Confusion is the "in the meantime" phase that your mind occupies until there is a distinct action you feel compelled to take. The moment when you feel you have figured things out. We want to move past things quickly, when in reality, what we are trying to move past quickly may have the answers that we have been hoping and praying to see."

Daughter's Perspective: It's frustrating when you can't get something, when you try, try, and try harder but still grapple with why things happen or what they mean. It's even more frustrating when you build the courage up to ask a question, and still don't understand.

Me to Mom: "Mom, I am trying to understand what you are saying, but some of this isn't sticking. It doesn't make sense to me that you have all of this wisdom but are just now beginning to use it in your own life."

Mom to Me: "*Knowing* what you should do is different than *doing* what you should do. It's easier to look at life and analyze it from the sidelines than doing what you should do in the moment. I don't want you to fall into the same pitfalls that I did so I am over explaining things. Everyone is an expert – until their life is examined to see if they are following what they preach. It's the miracle and mystery of life: How is it that you can have wisdom, but then choose actions that contradict with your hopes and dreams? Attachments to people, being comfort with the status quo and feeling obliged to help keep us stuck in situations. If you don't constantly remind yourself of what you want you will get complacent."

Me to Mom: "Is that why I sometimes want to give up?"

Mom to Me: "You want to give up because you can't explain what you are doing. You feel called to do more but you don't know where this road will lead. Things feel shaky now because you are operating on faith with no set path. You know that there could be some great things in your future but are unsure of what to do to make them happen. You think you need to do everything right now error free. In your mind, it feels easier to settle for what you know than to risk normalcy for what you don't know. You want to give up because you don't think you have what it takes to be successful."

"There is a difference between surrendering and giving up. Surrendering is knowing you don't have everything to be successful and asking for help; giving up implies that you have to do everything alone. Since the task is too big, you stop. The biggest obstacle to success is not the work or the time associated with the task; it is removing any belief that makes you feel as though you are not enough. When you surrender, you must also release what does not serve you. You will constantly be faced with resistance which is the byproduct of free will. Resistance shows up as inner conflict as you consider potential outcomes and the idea of failure. Free will or the ability to choose comes with a fear of judgment from others. Regardless of external pressures, you should find comfort in your ability to remain committed to the process of seeing it through.

When you remove from your mind everything that you think will come to you, good or bad, you are able to stay in the moment and concentrate on what is here right now."

"Every woman needs to hear that they are enough – whether they are eighteen, thirty-five, forty-five or sixty. Age does not imply ability; confidence in self is what motivates as well as the will to compete and believe that you can win."

"Every experience that we have in life comes with both opportunity and opposition. The bigger the experience, the greater the feelings and emotional investment. When the stakes are higher we often get intimidated. Knowing how to get past the point of hesitation is what gives you character and enables you to receive what is meant for you. There is never just one perfect plan in life; imperfection comes when you believe there is. When you force things to happen by ignoring what has been shown to you. When you tell yourself that this is the best you can do and settle for less. We are given multiple opportunities to get ourselves back into alignment with our goals. When things flare up, instead of attacking the interruption, or spending time on figuring out why it's there, stay grounded in your commitment to understanding – and in time you find answers."

Daughter's Revelation: And that is when she touched my shoulder and looked into my eyes. At that moment, I was the one with tears welling up, because I finally saw her point. I realize that I have spent too much time trying to be everything to everyone else, and not spending enough time giving to myself. Preoccupied with doing everything right, I have struggled to make decisions. I've been constantly afraid that I was going to do something wrong, since I was raised to follow the "rules," never questioning if these rules fit within my own life.

Me to Mom: "I know why we are here. You raised me as a good child, someone who is polite and giving, but it's time for me to grow up. Whatever reward I chased as a child, it is not enough to fill my soul as a woman. The dilemma I face now is that I know that my priorities need to change, but I am not sure how to change them. I am here to find out how to make the transition from your devoted daughter to a whole woman!"

Personal Belief Systems

Mom to Me: "You are not alone: that dilemma is what every person faces as they advance into adulthood. It is very common to feel as though you don't have what it takes – everyone, in fact, feels as if everyone else has the answers, and they themselves are struggling to keep up."

"If you want to make a change, you have to examine your Personal Belief Systems. Our Personal Belief Systems are what give our dreams a starting point to develop. We may have dreams and things we hope to achieve, but they have to start from a place of believing, a starting place of possibilities. That is where our beliefs come into being. Beliefs are not what we recite or read but but rather, they are the unspoken rules we follow. The messages that we replay in our mind. It is easy to figure out what a day will entail when someone is directing you, but when you have to figure it out yourself, you are forced to ask what it is that you believe in. It's the point when the assumptions that you have about life are played out in reality; when unknown things are projected and created."

"Belief in self is different from thinking that you are pretty or smart. Beliefs go into your core and examine your definitions: how do you see beauty, what makes you intelligent, what is the source of your knowledge. Thoughts form your decisions, becoming your starting point for what you allow to resonate in your body and dwell in your mind. Beliefs are different than what religion you choose or what types of things you invest in. It's a deeper perspective of what you think is possible, and how you are wired to deal with and address the things that come up. Situations in life grow and deflate over time, but what stays within your mind and spirit are those things that you hold within your emotional memory bank. If bad things have happened all of your life, you equate outcomes with trauma; if good things happened all of your life, you equate outcomes with celebrations. If you feel like nothing significant has happened in your life, you become satisfied with living an apathetic life. What you choose to pursue and what you allow in your personal space is a decision of commitment. What you choose to develop and what you choose to leave behind is a decision of awareness. Don't let hidden beliefs hold you back from what you wish to develop because you ignore them.

Also, don't let beliefs taint your mindset because you would rather operate blindly and from routine than out of rigor and understanding. Don't always believe what is told to you or what is shown to you but trust what inspires and draws your attention. Don't always believe what is communicated by the mainstream, or what the masses focus on. Thoughts are different than beliefs, because thoughts change and are based on feelings, perception and influence. You may have many thoughts about what happens, but there are only a few core beliefs: a belief in a higher power, the belief that life is guided by that higher power, a belief in goodness and a belief in your ability to operate in that goodness with others. Whenever thoughts conflict with your belief system, you owe it to yourself to understand where the misalignment occurred so that you can go back to that point and straighten out your thoughts. Don't let fleeting emotions take you away from your core – rather, concentrate on your beliefs, allowing that understanding to heal your thoughts."

Me to Mom: "How do I know a belief is true and worth believing in?"

Mom to Me: "There is a strong pull that touches us in a way that somehow, you don't know why it is there – but you know it is there, because it keeps coming back to you over and over again. It is a constant thought that shows up in various situations of your life. Beliefs allow you to endure life's troubles and random occurrences, giving you a sense of assurance. They are a natural inclination you have, a deep intuition. Knowing is a hard feeling to describe, because it is not based on something taught – or even experienced – it has more to do with your conviction as it relates to unexplainable things. When you believe, it is less about truth, and it is more about what is needed to get us through conflict. Believing is a choice to want to see hope and optimism, because you know that those are the only things that will motivate you to continue. Hope feeds into belief and turns our belief into a sense of being. Life gives us the mechanical structure to operate; beliefs give us the ability to feel and trust in things that we can't see. There is often a debate about religious beliefs – but just like God; love, hope, joy, and peace can't be see. But for them to work they require you to believe."

"Truth is a function of time as it relates to beliefs. If there is a belief that has been around for years, it's easier to accept because it has stood the test of time. In life, what you think you know is always tested. I used to avoid these tests because I didn't want to disrupt my foundation. I thought these tests would change my views but instead it refined my ability to decipher what I know from what I just chose to accept. To be still and know is to be able to believe without others trying to convince you. To have a sense of peace about things you can't explain is faith. In the same way we wake up with direction, our spirits also wake up knowing that there is something to be completed, a zest to experience life differently with more understanding. Through that understanding is how our beliefs are defined and supported. Knowing does not mean that we prove others' ways to be wrong so that our way will be right. It is accepting that there are multiple ways to achieve peace. Knowing is accepting that there is something better, and believing is using that knowledge to take action to make things better. Knowledge and knowing are often used interchangeably, but they are distinct and different. Knowledge is the collection of proven experiences, and knowing is the faith you place in your beliefs."

"I am bringing this up because there is a part of you that found comfort in proving to others you were right. It made you feel important and gave you an edge of arrogance. You are now seeking truth, but before, your whole existence depended on proving things to be right. Your need to be right created judgment and made you feel like you needed to control everything. You couldn't trust that life would be okay because without rules you expected things to fall apart. I need you to see that truth is what frees the spirit and not a fear of rules. Real truth brings peace to you and those around you – real truth heals."

Me to Mom: "I hear what you are saying, but there are challenging times that I face where I struggle to be motivated. How do I get through those times?"

Mom to Me: "If you feel you are always challenged, you have to ask yourself how challenges make you feel. Are these opportunities for you to experience new things and be stronger or do you feel whenever you are challenged, you will lose? Motivation is a matter of perspective. If you look at new things as good, then the outcome will be good. If you feel they are bad, then the outcome will be bad. The problem does not lie in what is going on, but in how you deal with challenge. Routine gives us a sense of comfort, in that we can predict how life will develop. The best way to deal with challenge is to *create* challenges in your life. Exercise is a great way to try different things in order to challenge your body so you remain flexible. Building relationships with others is another way that you can remain flexible, to see things from another's point of view. Remaining adaptable is your biggest defense against anger. Irritated people usually get their way so when faced with newness, they don't know how to deal and turn to defensiveness. They're mad at everyone – except for the one person who can change the situation: themselves."

"If you allow challenging times to make you feel intimidated and uncomfortable, it will lead to suffering. Constant suffering turns into a persistent state of unsettled resistance. Resistance is not always a bad thing. Going back to my exercise example, resistance training is used to build strength. If you look at life in the same way, it's a way through experiences. It is the time that it takes for you to be strong enough and limber enough to move with it, instead of letting it move against you. The best feeling is when you are able to get through a situation – and have understanding and peace."

"Peace is what we all want, what we all dream of, but often times we stay stuck in the constant replaying of our pre-programmed thoughts. Thoughts based on memories of who we used to be (shy, unenthused, and unengaged). Thoughts created from poor treatment and being ignored by people. Thoughts based on what people have told us. Even when our situation has changed, our minds maybe slow to catch up.

Affirmations speed up that process. By reminding ourselves of all of our good qualities and what we want we motivate ourselves to make better decisions. Decisions that create a new normal for life."

"If your new normal is health, you cook for yourself, create a balanced schedule and engage with other healthy people. If it is support, then you surround yourself with people who see your potential, date people that believe in you, and accept feedback. Peace is knowing that things will work. My mother used to tell me, "Everything works out in the end – so if it has not worked out, it is not the end." In peace you find the type of assurance that makes you feel like a new person – as it requires a new person to have a change in mindset."

Patience and Love

Me to Mom: "I feel like I have not spent enough time fully committed to living my best life and based on our conversation there are so many things I need to change. How quickly does change happen? How do I balance change with being patient?"

Mom to Me: "Some things are more immediate than others. When you eliminate something from your diet, you usually feel those effects within a few weeks. However the things you want: spiritual and emotional changes; takes more time and patience. Things such as stubbornness, inflexibility, procrastination and internal negative self talk takes longer to address. We often know we do it but others don't see these latent qualities. Patience with self and patience with life all involve time. How you use that time makes the difference. If you choose to lament on everything you are missing instead of what you want to gain you will become frustrated. Frustration stalls your progress. But if you choose to refocus that energy on something constructive – like thinking about how your life will improve you are repurposing that time."

"Patience is not just waiting, everybody has had to wait – we wait for planes, we wait in traffic, for food. Patience is not idling watching the time pass, it's holding onto the expectancy that great things can be done during this time. Remembering that life is meant to be good and giving God the necessary time to develop your blessings. Surrendering yourself to the process and using that time to work on you. Its trusting that things are happening behind the scenes. When even though you can't see what's changing, you know that things are working out. Things that will make what you want come true. The anticipatory energy you put forth triggers a complementary response, so that life can be fulfilled in ways unimaginable. Patience is devoting enough time to allow what has been triggered to develop."

"Patience is when you stop resisting the flow of life and allow things to just happen. When you are tired of fighting the natural flow of things and see time as a gift. When you use your time wisely. Instead of sulking about what you don't have you appreciate the opportunities that exist. Patience is realizing that timing is a mutual reward process. You have to be ready for the opportunity and the opportunity has to be developed. Many think that the key to life is working hard, but the truth of life lies in having something worth working hard for. Special blissful moments should be cherished. Patience is the time between those moments; the energy provided that sustains you until they happen again."

"Patience is the reassuring moment when there is a conscious internal shift, when you know you have changed for your own betterment. It's an atmosphere of reflection, when you realize the time spent was worth it and idle time is minimized. When what is most important rises to the top of our priorities and becomes a part of your life."

Me to Mom: "Everything you talk about involves love. God's love, self-love, and a love of experiences. It seems like everything we have discussed starts with love. When most people think of love it involves another person but how do you see love?"

Mom to Me: "Love has been misused, under acknowledged, and misunderstood. In its purest form, it isn't just an emotion but rather the way you allow life to move through you. It's an action, when you love, you are inspired to act. It the enabler of other emotions and activates forgiveness and compassion. It makes all experiences more enjoyable. Love is an acknowledgement that what you want can happen and a commitment to the process of receiving it. Love makes you accountable for personal growth so as opportunities arise you are able to take advantage of them. The process of developing what you didn't know that you needed, but are glad that you have."

"Once you love one person, you have capacity to love more because love allows you to see yourself in others. Love is contagious, when you are around love you can't help but to be happier. It's an opportunity to show your true self to another. When love is connected, the emotion is multiplied and feels intensified. It is an opening into a greater level of the goodness of life. Love is not a figment of your imagination, however you may feel you are living in a fairy tale because of the special feeling you have. The feeling of lightness and that anything is possible. Love is catalyst for awareness. When you love, you recognize love in more places and people can see it within you. Your senses come alive, and what used to be passive is now full of passion."

"Don't take love lightly, don't misuse love by saying it when you know your emotions don't support it. Love is meant to ignite truth, it is not meant to manipulate, control or make people question the integrity of the experience. Love is powerful, and love is a gift that everyone should experience. Love of life which is the enjoyment of experiences is the basis and the building block for love of another. Love builds on the elements observed in your life and serves as a foundation to extend it externally. Those elements include caring, respect, accountability, expression and flexibility. Love is misunderstood because people are chasing grandiose expressions of love, forgetting that the basics are necessary first."

"Misguided love can turn into envy. We experience envy when we want something that someone else has. The feeling comes from knowing that we are capable of having what others have. Envy will turn into bitterness and resentment if we don't use that initial feeling of envy to examine our life and pursue what we truly love. We must push our ego to make a change. Change may come in the form of figuring out what it is that we seek in our life. Usually it is more fulfillment, more meaning, or deeper connections. Envy is really is a signal, showing you what you want; it is up to you to figure out what you need to do to receive it. It is easier to blame your emotional distress on others but nothing improves. You have two choices: wallow in the feeling and take on the victim role, or wake up and ask yourself what it will take for you to seize this moment and get what you want. Positive and negative emotions are two sides of the same coin. Depending on the situation, hopelessness may turn to happiness, anger to acceptance, confusion to clarity, envy to love. The goal is to feel – and if you are able to feel without judgment, things that appear bad today may become better tomorrow. Time is a daily gift to see things through and compassion is a gift when we see things from another point of view. Two things necessary to have a proper perspective of love."

Me to Mom: "We have talked about so many things except the one area of my life that has caused me the most pain and confusion: Relationships."

Mom to Me: "You probably waited to talk about this because we never talked about relationships when you were growing up. I thought you were too young to really understand love and I wasn't ready to talk about my relationship with your father. He was a good man and we were in love. I fell in love with his humor, personality and love for family. He courted me and I enjoyed dating him before we married. We wanted you and were happy when I got pregnant. You were not the reason why our marriage failed. Our problems didn't stem from a lack of love but from a lack of accountability. He didn't know how to show up for our family in the relationship. He was dealing with a lot of stuff that had nothing to do with me that prevented him from being present. I needed him to be emotionally available and be able to meet the needs of our family. I needed him to fully commit to being a husband and father. I overlooked some things when we dated because I was in love and I thought love would be enough to overcome anything in our marriage. We divorced because I felt that if I was doing everything by myself I didn't need to be married to him. I divorced him but he never divorced being your father and cherished that role. Even though our marriage didn't work, I never regretted the experience or having you. Your life and seeing you grow up to be such an amazing person has made everything in my life worthwhile. I didn't bring this up before because I remarried when you were very young. I wanted you to have a strong relationship with your step-father, which you did. I married your step-father because I knew he would be a committed father. But now I see through our conversation that you needed me to talk about this and shed light on my relationships."

Me to Mom: "I needed to hear you say that. I needed to know that I was wanted. I needed to understand what happened in your first marriage. Thank you for putting the pieces together. For years, I questioned how my life began and the circumstances surrounding my birth. I felt like my relationship with my biological father was never defined and I've struggled to make any man accountable in my life. I easily play the friend role since I am a giver. But rarely have gotten to play the leading lady and that bothers me, because I want more. Relationships have always been a big mystery to me. My timing is off as well as my ability to read the signs. I know I need help in this area. I feel like I am ready for a relationship but struggle with how to get in one. In your opinion how do you know when it's time for a relationship? How will I know that I am ready?"

Mom to Me: "Love is difficult for many people; don't feel like you are the only one going through this. A lot of my love lessons were through trial and error so don't feel bad if you think you made a mistake. Love is bigger than just romantic love, it is a universal gift you give to everybody. Forgiveness, generosity, care and compassion should not be reserved for special relationships but should be extended to everyone. Romantic relationships are a choice; an intimate decision to be with someone when you allow yourself to be vulnerable and accessible. Romantic relationships build on the close bonds of friendships. The timing of romantic relationships is hard to predict, because it involves two beings, choosing to be together. The opportunity must be met with openness for there to be magic. Often, when you are the one single girl in the crew, you may think that your time has passed or that romance is not for you. Patience and trust is needed for good relationships; those that have meaning and purpose."

"You shouldn't just strive for a state of being, such as to 'be in a relationship' or to 'be engaged' or to 'be married'. Being in a relationship does not imply you are happy; you can have the title without the feelings that make a relationship meaningful. The emotions surrounding those statements are what add passion and feelings to those statements. You should strive for a deep connection, and hope the other person wants to know you fully and still chooses to be with you. The intention behind relationships is the foundation from which everything else is born. If two people come together out of insecurity, pain, frustration or loneliness, that spirit will be what surrounds everything that is done in the relationship. If you are not honest about where you are personally you won't truly know what you are projecting."

"Relationships were never meant to harm us, nor were they ever meant to stifle our spirit. So many people think that in order to be with another, they must stop being themselves, which is so untrue. Romantic love is not about taking care of or saving someone. It's about coming together with a goal to see both of you grow into better individual people. With everything, balance is important, and relationships are no different. You have to understand what you can handle. 'Handle' is an important thing to consider, because although there is so much good that comes from a relationship, there is a sacrifice. There is a sacrifice of personal time and personal space, but you gain the opportunity to share. The most loving relationships make you feel as though you are not alone. For most ladies, we expect that when we are ready we will be able to wave a magical wand and the perfect man will appear. Relationships involve compromises in how you communicate, how you spend your time and how you incorporate the other person into your life. If you are someone who likes 'private me time,' a relationship may feel like an invasion; if you are someone who finds it hard to communicate, you may have to learn how to express your thoughts and feelings better. Knowledge of self, and knowing what you want, are both imperative for meaningful relationships. You will know when it is time – and until then, you will know what is most important to work on."

"Love for me has been my greatest lesson, and my greatest source of pain. Love wasn't the problem; how I looked at it was. When I was growing up, I thought if I had a relationship, I would have everything. I thought marriage was the ultimate reward. My mother's friends and everyone from the church put marriage on the same level as the Virgin Mary. You had two choices: become a nun, or commit yourself to someone who could legitimize your existence. So that is what I did: I got married young, only to realize that marriage is not the climax of life. I thought I would be the envy of my friends and feel like my life was complete. I thought I would feel whole when I changed my name – and it would finally make me feel confident. I quickly found out that life doesn't stop when you change your last name. I was so preoccupied with what I needed to do to keep love that I forgot what it took for me to attract love – and that was being me. You are put on this earth to figure out your gift, and once you know what it is, it's your job to share it. There are so many frustrated wives and mothers who find that marriage does not fulfill them – they think they have fallen out of love with their mates, but they have really fallen out of love with themselves. It took me years, decades, to rebuild my lost self; it took me years to remember who I was before marriage took over."

"I was so hard on you because you have a vulnerable spirit. Vulnerability is not a bad thing, until it is met with manipulation. You like to see the good in people, and we all have good, but often the good in people doesn't prevail because they let ulterior motives take over. I never thought love was a bad thing, but I know firsthand what can happen to young girls who get into relationships that they are not ready to deal with. I was that young girl. I had to learn how to stand up and deal with the maturity that comes with balancing the needs of another. I had to develop strength to say no, compassion to use the word yes, be smart enough to know when to compromise and be self-aware to know when to leave. There is no exact book on what someone needs to do or say when you are in love; you respond based on the situation and what you want. What you want will change over time, and what you will be willing to deal with changes based on what you are willing to sacrifice. Love, just like life, has no hard-and-fast rules. The only rule is to know yourself, love yourself and be open to let others in. If you can do that, while maintaining the spirit that is within you, then I feel you have found an ideal situation: one in which you can thrive and grow, but also one where the real you can just be. You are too special and unique to be lost in love."

Daughter Reflection: Things seem to make more sense about why I'm still single. I want love and want to be married but my biggest fear is having to dim my light for the sake of another. I have seen many women downplay their goals to support their mates. Or suppress an outgoing personality so they don't outshine their mate when they go out. I am working hard to have a voice; I can't silence it now since I am so close to using it.

Me to Mom: "I am usually the giver in relationships and give sometimes without being asked. As you mentioned I am vulnerable and often feel used – what do I need to do to address this?"

Mom to Me: "If you always selflessly give without communicating your needs, you may be creating one sided relationships. If you find yourself in these situations a lot then it is more about you than the other person. To address this, and anything that concerns you, you must examine your life – see if there are repeat patterns – and ask yourself why you maintain something that bothers you. You can't ignore the feeling or wish it to go away. The moment a problem arises, the solution also appears if you are willing to accept the truth. There will be times in your life where it will be easier to blame your misfortune on someone else. But the true sign of maturity is the moment when you stop looking for excuses – but, instead, elevate your thinking. If you wish to have better relationships, you create them by expressing what you want – and treating others the way you want to be treated. If you want more balance, you have to speak up and advocate for yourself before you feel taken advantage of. You show people how you want to be treated. It's best to address this before others assume that victim and doormat are the only roles you can play. No one is a mind reader, you have to actively work on it in order for others to see you differently and for you to get used to accepting more."

Me to Mom: "If we all have a need to be loved and want our needs to be met in relationships, why it is so hard to ask for help?"

Mom to Me: "Needs make us human and asking for help is a part of life. How you address needs says a lot about your character. Will you be a constant user, relying on others to fill every void? Will you be a pinch-hitter, never fully committing to one thing, but running from activity to activity to feel useful? Will you be the defensive one who lies about needing help and criticizes others for their vulnerability? Or will you choose to handle it responsibly – finding a constructive way to admit what you need, doing what you can do, accepting help and trusting others? If you take the necessary time to figure out a sustainable, constructive way to fill your needs, you create depth. If you take the first step toward filling that need, you create strength – and if you continue to fill yourself first, you create confidence. Strength does not come from exercising good judgment one time; it comes from a series of events that define your behavior. The key to help is to appreciate it when it is given. Appreciation comes from understanding and recognizing the effort. You won't always be in control and able to do what you want and that is okay, we are here to help each other. To know that you are capable while allowing others to do things on your behalf is the true form of partnership. It's a partnership because you respect the effort that it takes because you have done it before and are willing to reciprocate."

Me to Mom: "So when will I be ready for love?"

Me to Mom: "There is a time and season for everything, and people move through stages at different times. The timing of relationships is based on your ability to be vulnerable and open with another. Get over the need to prove how good you are for the other person. Instead focus on strengthening the special connection you share. Authentic love creates bonds without restricting our individual creativity. Relationships, like all human interactions, are external reflections of yourself – walking examples of what you believe. If you feel as though your time has passed, and that you will be alone, then you subconsciously cut off your ability to attract. If you believe that relationships are difficult, then that is what you will receive. Every thought or dream is projected in love; your partner is a walking mirror of what you hold to be true and how you see yourself. The best relationships allow for worries to be seen without judgment and assistance to be given without obligation. Your mindset, emotional maturity and openness are the greatest predictors of relationship readiness. People come together at different points in their life, but the opportunity for success is much better when you know yourself, love yourself and are open to someone else's opinion and presence. There has to be room for the other to grow and develop, and there has to be room for you both to develop as a couple."

Me to Mom: "With all of this talk of love, do you believe in soul mates? Is there someone designed for each of us?"

Mom to Me: "When you expose your truest self, then I believe that your truest self will be reflected back to you. Your perspective on life shapes what you see in life. If you are happy, you will gravitate to the first signs of happiness; if you are sad, you will see that first. Life is a reflection of what we choose to see. The question is not so much if soul mates exist, but are we able to see that they exist. To see them is more about our ability to own our own experience, and live in full expression to be seen, rather than waiting for someone to tell us that we are enough, and worthy to be with them. That happens when you are ready to show up 100% in all aspects of life, and be your purest form of love – able to give your gifts and operate out of generosity. When you are standing confidently in every experience, without shame or personal judgment, then the person of your dreams appears because you have become the person that you dream of. Striving for something and achieving it allows you to respect and give yourself permission to honor that same experience when you see it in another. You understand what it took for them to get to that point, because you had a similar journey. Your soul mate is a combination of who you see in your dream, your interests and your future."

"The process for soul mate attraction is less about dating and looking the part, and more about playing an authentic role in your own life. The unscripted life, the life that you design and create is the only role that you should ever play. Once you do that, the love that you create is what will come to be. It's an inner feeling that pulls two people together, and drives chance meetings and conversations to happen. You may not do anything directly to get the other person but they are instead drawn to you because of how you handle your own life. Your generosity, sense of loyalty, the love you give to your family and how you treat others. Your spirit has everything to do with what happens – it is the projection of your being that makes others want to come towards you and be around you."

"Soul mate connections are special, so when they happen it is best to show your appreciation right in that moment. Saying thank you is only one part of it, expressing emotion is the second part. Appreciation recognizes that the feeling is unique to this moment and person. Acknowledge that it feels good to be seen and then being able to fully see the other person. When these experiences happen, it is good to communicate your feelings so others are aware of how you felt in the moment. A direct way of letting others know that you see value in the interaction. That the shared experience is unique to them and special. An exchange of energy is what drives the cohesiveness in soul mate relationships. If your energy and your feelings are not expressed on a grand level, it means you are withholding parts of yourself that your soul mate needs to see to come alive. Soul mates are each other's catalysts for awakening their hearts because they relate on a similar level. Often knowing what to say or do because they have the same emotional makeup and wounds. The ability to forgive someone that is like you allows you to in turn forgive yourself. This comfort gives people a reason to believe in love again and restores lost dreams. You have at least three major loves. The first helps you identify love, the second shows you what you need in love and with the third you learn how to appreciate love. I believe a person has more than one soul mate. They come to us when we least expect it and are sent to heal. Soul mates can turn into more if both people are ready for deeper commitment. If not, it doesn't minimize the relationship; both are forever connected and better for the experience. Love is never lost, it may change but the hearts are always joined. Don't think just because you are single you have not been in love or met one of you soul mates. You are relationship material. You just have to relax, fully engage, enjoy the process and let it naturally flow."

Daughter's Reflection: Mom makes love sound logical so why do I feel like it makes me illogical? Once I let a guy into my life I fall hard and it's difficult to move on. I know what it's like to be hurt so I don't want to add to their pain by walking away. Waiting on someone to figure out what they want makes my happiness contingent on theirs; which isn't fair. For others to treat me differently, I have to ask for what I need and believe I can receive it.

Mom to Me: "What else do you need to know? I am an open book, and we are not burdened by time, so we can speak from the heart. You have an opportunity that not many have: the access to wisdom without fear. You have the opportunity to ask and receive anything you ever wanted in this dream state. You have been given the freedom to go within and access feelings you weren't comfortable addressing before. Dreams are created by the dreamer and give us a sense of control that we often lack in reality. They allow us to change time and by doing that we can go back to simpler points in our life. They give us a safe place to deal with things and achieve the closure we need."

Me to Mom: "I am in awe of your wisdom, love and advice. We have covered so many topics and I can honestly say my soul is full. You gave me the answers I needed and I feel complete. I am speechless. Thank you mom. I love you."

Daughter's Reflection: I look up at her face and she looks happy. She has a glow unlike anything I have ever seen– a peace that is not present when we talk in this lifetime. She has always been a good mother but our conversation makes her feel like my best friend. I have always loved my mother but now our connection is much deeper. In her infinite wisdom, she grounded me in truth and gave me timeless advice. I just gazed at her, feeling her warmth of spirit and love.

Mother's Reflection: As I look at my daughter, I am overcome by the experience and by my emotions. I am confident that my daughter will be fine, and I feel like I have done my job as a mother. We connected in a common place of understanding, and only received goodness. In this place, what was most important was the exchange, and my ability to stay with her, hear what she was saying and not let anything stop or prevent me from sharing in this moment in order to help her.

Everything Will Work Out Fine

Mom to Me: "Don't worry if your milestones happen later or differently than your friends. Things develop as you develop. When I say everything will work out fine, it is a statement that comes from a higher place of understanding. When confronted with setbacks and feeling like my dreams won't come true; I change my focus. I acknowledge what I am feeling while also giving my anxiety something to do. I take a walk, workout, write a letter or work on a hobby. When you see results in one area of your life, problems seem more manageable because you remind yourself that you are able. I have to believe things will change, because what I choose to see appears. There is a beauty in changing your focus; it makes our biggest fears disappear. We may still have them but seem small in comparison to the other things in your life. When times get tough I focus on my blessings in life and it reassures me that tomorrow will be better."

Me to Mom: "You say that everything will work out fine, but why am I struggling to take in everything that you have told me? We have talked about so many things, and I feel as though this conversation is coming to an end – and I am not ready to have this part of you leave me. Why am I struggling to hold on to everything you have said? I want to trust and believe your words, but I am also frustrated, because I feel when I wake up, things will go back to the way they were. And I don't want them to."

Mom to Me: "I know you feel overwhelmed, and that doubt is a common emotion that comes with change, but I also know that you are a part of me – and if you think I am strong and capable of doing everything, then you should feel the same way about yourself. You are my little dreamer, the one who used to daydream more than going outside to play. You are the creative one – you astound me with your ability to see something, and then go out and make it. You are also my worrier, overthinking everything. You thought you had to be my mini-me growing up and tried to take care of anything you thought I wasn't doing. When you were a girl you were an old soul, mature and wise behind your years, and now that you are growing up it's time to give yourself a little bit of slack, have some fun, do silly things, take risks."

"Your foundation is so solid that even if you do something that is shocking, everyone including yourself should give you a pass because you have always acted with integrity. Growing up you said I was strict, which was true; but you also were so disciplined that my rules just reinforced how you already looked at things. You always wanted me to know how good you were, and that you wouldn't do the things your older siblings did. I wondered if you ever did things you wanted to do or if you were just focused on what not to do all the time. This time in your life is what you will need for your own balance. If you want to take chances, take chances. If you want to do something without my permission, do it and don't tell me. If you want to dance, take classes. You have a blank slate, and you own what things you will put on your canvas. Now is your time. I gave you the tools you needed as a child; now you have to combine those things with your intuition and go out and experience all of life. No more excuses. No more judgment. No more fear!"

"You are a woman, a strong woman, a woman I respect and admire. I am learning from you just as much as you think you are learning from me. Stop thinking about everything that could go wrong, and trust that things will be fine. You allowed yourself to have this experience – and look how good you feel. Trust that this experience will not leave you and know that I will never leave you. I am your parent and I love you. If you fear I will leave you, you believe this about everyone. If divorcing your father made you feel rejected I am sorry. Instead of focusing on his absence think about everyone that stepped in to fill the gap. You can't live expecting people to always leave. If you do, you will constantly push people away before they have a chance to do it to you. There is no set expiration date on relationships so stop trying to predict when they will end. Stop thinking that you can't hold onto things or people you love. You have to stop believing that men will disappoint you. Your preoccupation with this fear is making you miss out on life. If you really want your dreams to come true you have to cherish what you have now. You have everything you need, you just have to believe it and act on it. You don't have to be alone; let people in and let them love you."

The Resolution

Daughter's Reflection: Just as my mother says those words, she closes her eyes and then asks me to close mine and tell her what I see. I see an ocean, a blue ocean with strong waves; this image of vacation calms me. I have been swept to a place that allows me to rest and I am able to let it all go. I release any misunderstandings, my views of a broken past and the stigma I have carried of not feeling wanted. I take a deep sigh of relief; I am now ready to enjoy this vacation. Vacations have always symbolized a celebration. I think that is why mom travels so much. It is her way to celebrate life. As I close my eyes, I feel a huge sense of completeness, knowing that all I just heard will help me. I will stop analyzing everything, appreciate each moment and start living without rules. It's time for me to have fun and stop worrying about what will happen.

Since being in Peru, I am much more aware of nature. When I hear the birds flying over my head, it reminds me of walks I used to take when I was a little girl; there is commonness that animals give you. No matter the time or place, they can bring you back to what's familiar, the things that are always present – just like a Mother's love. The butterflies and the smell of the outdoors reassure me that nature is my home, a place that I initially pushed away but that now feels comfortable. It's funny how you can have an out-of-body experience, but also feel as though things are happening to you at that very moment. Life gives us what we need when we are ready to receive it. Peru is a magical place, one that invites and stimulates your soul; a place where you are able to be yourself and see opportunities within. This place make you want to love, forgive and seek understanding. We all are works in progress; Peru is the place where life can be accepted and not judged.

How many mothers and daughters have this moment to bond, share and go back to simpler times? This conversation was a mix of everything that I was afraid to ask, with what I wish I had known, seasoned with the things I have always wanted to hear from my mother. I always knew that she loved me, but sometimes I didn't feel as if she saw me as an individual. Now I know that she cared for me, so that I would have a strong sense of life and a strong sense of my own sense of belonging and self-purpose.

Although marriage is a beautiful thing, she didn't want me to think that it was my only option. She wanted me to be exposed to many experiences so that I could choose what I wanted, rather than feeling that my possibilities were limited. I know I am enough, because I was enough of a reason for her to leave situations that she knew I couldn't deal with. I was worthy because she has held me in the depths of her being from the beginning. Mothers have everything they need to create life in the physical and emotional sense. Not all mothers choose to have biological children; some choose to nurture others' kids, animals or mentor. It's the spirit of a woman that makes her a mother, not biology. Daughters are their greatest creation, their most cherished gift and their biggest lesson sent. My mother whispered everything into my ear that I had hoped she would ever say. She knew what I needed to hear to erase my deep regrets and disappointments. She reminded me that everything was fine, and would turn out well. We ended our conversation in the same way it began, two innocent spirits engaged in a spiritual exchange. One could say that this was make-believe, and was never to occur in real life, but it was a different experience that I can't explain. All I can say is that I needed this in my life, and that it was worth the time to come and receive what my soul was looking for. A trip to Peru completed my development in life.

My mother has always been wise beyond her years. It didn't matter what happened in her life because wisdom is timeless and never dies. Her truth and love were constant and sparked something within me. She was and became what she always has been. Time nor decisions, hurt or perceived setbacks took away what was created in her and what she was to become. Life doesn't change in the way we think it does. Love is replayed in various scenes and moments of time, and regardless of what we go through, the pureness of love remains in us all.

I was surprised that mom showed up in my dream and not my grandmother. I have always looked at my grandmother as the quintessential sign of motherhood. I idolized her because she spoiled me. She was always attentive to my needs and spent her time loving on me. She saw my potential and accepted me for who I was. She was not only my "Grandmommy," she was everyone's "Grandmommy," playing the "big mama" role, but she was far from looking dull, unkempt or frumpy. Everything she did supported keeping a great home, but she never looked homely, often accessorizing sequins with leather and fur. She was my definition of unconditional love, and she has been that for me for so many years, both during my formative years and as I grew into an adult. So to be visited by my mother in a dream, and see her being everything that my grandmother represented to me, surprises me – but it also nurtures me in a way that heals my way of thinking. This experience has taught me that there are no wrong or right things. That to judge things as right or wrong only places us in a box, a box full of limitations. But if you open yourself up, you will receive whatever you need to be healed. Forgiveness only materialized when I changed my perception of what I allowed myself to see. I know something had to shift within my mother to even allow for this experience to happen, and something had to change within me.

For all the time and energy I spent on analyzing her every decision, and how she lived her life, I have to admit that we are more similar than different. She showed me more in her actions than her words. She showed me that you can have fullness in life and be fulfilled. Romantic love is not the only love you can have – you can be in love with life, and that is okay. She taught me that I am enough, and capable of being my own biggest advocate and provider. Mom was strong enough to create her own road and follow her direction; she is the gypsy and I have become her copycat. A chameleon who finally pushed for what she wanted – who has now found comfort in being the architect of her self-created life.

Peru is where I saw my mother as a woman; a woman with stories, emotions and a full being, rather than just being a person I turn to when in need. Here in the Sacred Valley I experienced real love, and I will be forever changed and grateful for this experience. It is a place full of miracles. As I move forward with my life, I know I am ready and equipped with knowing what it takes to create strong bonds, express love and live a joyful life. I am ready because I have had the best example to follow, and I now know everything that has made this woman so wise. I am able to create what mom has given me: the ability to grow, opportunities to learn, and experiences to fully engage and live. I reconnected with the best parts of both of us and learned how to live as an adult.

A wise person once told me that you know you are at peace when you have no response, no anger, no sadness, but a state of calm. Calm demonstrates that there is no subliminal control, and that you no longer feel compelled to respond. Calmness within all relationships is the goal. Calmness between a mother and daughter is the only way the relationship will withstand its evolving stages. By allowing a mother to vent frustrations and feelings surrounding the events of her daughter's life, the daughter better understands her mother. And for the mother to understand her daughter, she must try to ignore their topics of disagreement, and focus more on the type of woman she raised, seeking understanding behind the motivation of the action. When someone can fully recognize the headspace surrounding decisions, and remember similar times in their own lives, they can speak out of compassion instead of conflict.

There is no more to say, there is no more to do. I can just move on now, keeping her innocence in my heart, with my mother keeping mine in hers. I think that the purpose of this trip and the reason why we are both here is for us to learn to ignore all other stimuli, and become each other's single point of focus. Not in the same way that a mother does with a newborn baby, responding to obvious needs, but taking the time to really get to know each other's emotional blueprint. Some people will think this is just a young woman with a strong imagination, but I know this is something bigger. It's a dream that has come true, a real connection of two hearts in time. I am thankful.

"Excuse me, miss, are you ready to go?" I am not familiar with this voice, and when I wake up, I see the tour guide walking towards me. It feels like I have been here for days, but the tour guide tells me we have only been here for an hour. It is time to explore other parts of the Sacred Valley. This is just the first stop of many stops on the tour. I feel discombobulated, not remembering where I am or what is going on. As I fully open up my eyes, I see my mother walking towards me wearing the black jumpsuit she had on this morning. Seeing her face immediately reassures me and makes me feel at peace. She asks me what I have been doing, because she has tried to call me several times. I look down at my phone and see that I have several missed calls from her. To avoid having to answer her question, I suggest we take a picture to capture this moment. I put my arm around her, and raise the other hand to take a selfie. The sun blinds my ability to see our reflection in the screen, so after I snap the picture I go back to see how we look. The first thing that grabs my attention is our eyes. Since I suffer from allergies, my eyes are often swollen, but their current state is not a reaction to an irritant but an emotional response to a healing. My mother shares my expression: eyes that are slightly puffy and red, combined with big smiles. The looks on our faces are not looks of sadness but of bliss – we are smiling so hard that there is little space for our eyes, which in any event are squinting from the hot sun on our faces. Mom is the first to speak, and she asks me if

I am all right. Instead of responding, I reach over and give her a big hug as I whisper "Yes" in her ear. We both let out a big sigh of relief and hold hands; joined together as we move forward to make all of our dreams come true.

Made in the USA
Columbia, SC
01 December 2020